Forgotten Songs and Stories of the Sea

For my sister; my first mate

Forgotten Songs and Stories of the Sea

A Treasury of Voices from our Maritime Past

Caroline Rochford

PEN & SWORD
HISTORY

First published in Great Britain in 2016 by
Pen & Sword History
an imprint of
Pen & Sword Books Ltd
47 Church Street
Barnsley
South Yorkshire
S70 2AS

ISBN 978 1 47387 865 5

A CIP catalogue record for this book is available from the British
Library

Typeset in Ehrhardt by
Mac Style Ltd, Bridlington, East Yorkshire
Printed and bound in the UK by CPI Group (UK) Ltd,
Croydon, CR0 4YY

Pen & Sword Books Ltd incorporates the imprints of Pen & Sword
Archaeology, Atlas, Aviation, Battleground, Discovery, Family
History, History, Maritime, Military, Naval, Politics, Railways,
Select, Transport, True Crime, and Fiction, Frontline Books, Leo
Cooper, Praetorian Press, Seaforth Publishing and Wharncliffe.

For a complete list of Pen & Sword titles please contact
PEN & SWORD BOOKS LIMITED
47 Church Street, Barnsley, South Yorkshire, S70 2AS, England
E-mail: enquiries@pen-and-sword.co.uk
Website: www.pen-and-sword.co.uk

Contents

Introduction

The Age of Sail was an era that lasted two and a half centuries, from the late 1500s to the mid 1800s. This was a time when great sailing ships voyaged between the continents, carrying passengers and valuable cargoes from one nation to another. Merchant adventurers had established a vast network of trading links across the seas, serving to make this period of history a bold and prosperous one; yet it was also an era of seemingly endless naval conflicts. State-of-the-art warships were constructed, enormous fleets were mustered and the oceans were transformed into boundless battlegrounds as the richest countries vied against each other to become supreme rulers of the waves. England, France, America, Spain and the Netherlands were key players in many of these wars; and as the centuries passed, history books were filled with awe-inspiring tales of heroism and sheer barbarism at sea. Inevitably, as Horatio Nelson, Napoleon Bonaparte, Sir Francis Drake and the other great naval personalities passed away, scholars' archives were confined to library shelves and the memories of these glorious sea battles faded with the passage of time.

William Cox Bennett was a nineteenth-century English poet and staunch patriot who lamented the fact that his country's maritime history was being forgotten by the younger generations. To remedy this, he composed a number of verses commemorating Britain's triumphs, in the hope that his beloved country's days of naval dominance would be remembered and celebrated by the whole nation, particularly the next generation of sailors in the Royal Navy.

Other Victorian writers were inspired by the beauty and romance of the sea, and penned their own commemorative poems, many of which were published in contemporaneous newspapers and magazines. This book introduces modern readers to a selection of these long-forgotten maritime melodies, along with fascinating tales drawn from the annals of naval history, as reported in the British press so many years ago. Through accounts of mythical sea creatures, quaint seaside traditions, swashbuckling pirates and ambitious naval inventions, *Forgotten Songs and Stories of the Sea* offers a glimpse of a bygone age when voyagers explored the high seas and their loved ones were left behind to wonder if they'd ever see their brave sailor men and women again.

♪ *What do the Wild Waves Say?* ♪

S.W.H.

Printed in *The Leicester Chronicle & Leicestershire Mercury*, 30 July 1887

'What do the wild waves say,
What do the wild waves say,
Oh! tell me sailor, tell me pray,
What do the waves, the wild waves say?'

Oft have I stood upon the sand,
And watched the ocean charge the land.
And often have I longed to know
What meant that strange mysterious flow.

So grand, so glorious, so free,
There's nothing like the rolling sea,
It always seemeth unto me
The mirror of the Deity.

When tempest brood, and thunders roar,
And foam-capped billows lash the shore,
I love to stand and watch the sea,
In all its dread sublimity.

'Oh! sailor, thou hast known the deep,
Say do the billows laugh or weep,
Do they peal forth a merry strain,
Or chant they forth some sad refrain?'

The sailor turned to me and smiled,
Then pointed to the watery wild,
'The waves,' he cried, 'they speak to me
Of some dim, vast eternity.

'They rolled back in the ages past,
Ere man did on the earth reside,
And when mankind shall pass away,
Still on shall boom that restless tide.

'Cities may crumble into dust,
And empires fall into decay,
But still around the continents
The sea shall toss its snow-white spray.

'The swiftest steamer it can wreck,
The stoutest ironclad it can sink,
The crashing shot, that shakes the rock,
Falls harmless on its glassy brink.

'For loving hearts have waited long,
And loved and waited all in vain;
The sea has swallowed up their hopes,
And rent the dearest links in twain.'

The sailor bowed his head and wept,
Then stretched his hand toward the sea,
'Ye dark relentless waves,' he cried
'Give back my treasures unto me.'

  The waves come thundering on the beach,
And seemed to hiss with savage glee,
'Thy treasures sailor now are ours,
We will not give them back to thee.'

But through a deep rift in the clouds,
The bright moon burst with sudden glow,
'Sailor thy treasures are in heaven,'
We heard a sweet voice murmur low.

And still the winds that swept the bay,
Seemed to be whispering in their play
The burden of my plaintive lay:
'What do the wild waves say,
What do the wild waves say,
Oh! tell me sailor, tell me pray,
What do the waves, the wild waves say?'

3

The Adventures of a Girl Sailor-Boy

On Monday, 3 November 1902, a remarkable story was heard at the Bristol police court. The person in the dock was 15-year-old Esther McEwan, who stood before the Bench wearing a shabby suit of men's clothes. Her hair was shorn and she looked decidedly miserable as she listened to PC Townsend giving evidence against her.

Earlier that morning he'd been patrolling the streets when he heard a group of men talking about a woman, disguised as a man, receiving payment for working aboard the cargo ship *Gem*, which had just arrived at Bristol Harbour. The curious constable went to investigate, and eventually came across a gathering of sailors outside the Board of Trade offices, waiting for payment. Amongst them was the prisoner, Miss McEwan, who was due to collect £1 5s 4d. As soon as PC Townsend began to question the young sailor 'boy', she burst into tears and admitted that she was really a girl.

The child was an orphan who lived with her older sister in Wishart, near Glasgow, but was cruelly treated, so one day she ran away from home. Faced with the prospect of having to find her own way in the world, Esther decided she'd fare better as a man. She cut off her long, dark hair and secured herself a more masculine outfit. She already had a thickset build, and made such a convincing boy that she had no trouble at all in obtaining employment at a nearby colliery. There she worked as a trolley boy, pushing the heavy coal-laden carts to the surface. She went about her duties just like all the other men without arousing any suspicion. Though she enjoyed the camaraderie at the colliery, she'd always yearned for a life on the ocean wave. She loved nothing more than escaping into a romantic novel, and one day, having read the story of an unhappy young girl who dressed as a boy and ran away to sea, Esther was inspired to do the same.

In September 1901, after four months underground, she handed in her notice and left for Dundee, where she found work as a cabin boy on board a coasting steamer, *Discovery*. She laboured under the pseudonym Allan Gordon, and later joined the crew of a ship bound for Valparaíso, Chile. Her third voyage was aboard the *Gem*, where she worked as a messroom steward, serving food and drinks to the officers.

Nobody suspected anything until the ship reached Alexandria, Egypt, where each crew member was obliged to undergo a routine examination by a doctor. Knowing she'd be discovered, Esther was forced to admit her sex to the captain. She fully expected to be punished for her deception, but to her

surprise, the captain took pity on her. He agreed to keep her secret and take her back to Britain as a passenger.

The fact that the messroom steward had been confined to 'his' cabin for the duration of the return voyage without any explanation was a hot topic of discussion among the rest of the crew, and wild theories soon began to circulate. It was one of these conversations that PC Townsend had overheard, which led to Esther's arrest.

The magistrate's clerk, upon hearing how much the prisoner had relished her time at sea, asked her why she hadn't considered finding work as a stewardess. She responded by saying that nobody would employ a stewardess with short hair, so she'd have to wait until it grew back before any such opportunity came along. The Bench asked if she'd consider returning to her sister's custody in the meantime, but the prisoner refused point blank.

Esther McEwan was duly charged with 'wandering abroad without any visible means of subsistence', and not being under proper control. She was handed into the care of a local housekeeper, provided with feminine clothing and given a position as a domestic servant – a career deemed much more appropriate for a young working-class woman, no matter how spirited she was.

The 'First' Female Sea Captain

In the nineteenth century, French sailors had a reputation for being particularly superstitious. They believed it was bad luck to bring a woman on board a ship, for women, they said, were the cause of many disasters. In a twist of irony, the honour of being 'the only woman sea captain in the world' was bestowed upon a lady named Maria Joanna Kersaho, who died in France in 1901, aged 72. When she was 12 years old she used to go to sea with her father, himself a sea captain. She took the helm after his death, and went on to captain three vessels of her own. During her career, as reported by the *Gloucestershire Echo* on 7 October 1901, she was awarded several naval medals, as well as prize money, in recognition of 'her heroism on the water'.

However, there were other contenders for the title of 'the only woman sea captain in the world'. In 1890, according to *The Worcestershire Chronicle*, a female sea captain named Miss Hannah Millar died at Saltcoates, North Ayrshire, aged 82. In her younger days she was the commander of the brig

Clitus, a position inherited from an elder sister, who'd held this rank for over thirty years.

The girls' father was a merchant who'd built the brig from the timber of a wrecked man-of-war. After his death, the elder Miss Millar took over the business and sailed between Scotland and Ireland, successfully 'managing all the business of freight, cargo, and ship's stores' whilst commanding her own crew. She died in 1862, leaving command of the *Clitus* to her younger sister.

Germany's first female sea captain qualified in 1939. Her name was Fraulein Anneliese Sparbier, who was described by *The Sunderland Echo and Shipping Gazette* as a 'good-looking, brown-haired, young girl' who was actually a school teacher, but her love of the sea, coupled with a desire to travel the world, gave her the determination to train to become a captain.

♪ The Ship's Company ♪

Frederic E. Weatherly
Printed in *Family Magazine*, 1890

She's the captain of the *Waterwitch*,
And a very good captain too,
And she's trim and neat from her hat to her feet,
And her eyes are blue – true blue.
And whenever we meet upon the shore
Or sailing across the bay,
I cry, 'Boat ahoy!' like a true sailor boy,
And this is what I say:
'Oh, make me your boa's'n or your mate,' say I,
'And let me sail with you,
For you are the captain of the *Waterwitch*,
And a very good captain too.'

Then she lifts her eyes with sweet surprise:
'The mate, that sails with me,
Must honour and obey, and never say me nay,
On land or on the sea.'
'Then I'll be your mate, sweetheart,' say I
(And she gives me her pretty hand),
'For I want no more on land or shore
Than to live at your command.'
So I beg to state, she's made me mate,
And together we sail the blue,
For she is the captain of the *Waterwitch*,
And I – am all the crew.

Sydney Cowell

Mary Pelham and the Fair-Haired Sailor

In January 1923, a grisly murder made the national headlines: a middle-aged woman of an 'unfortunate class' had been murdered, leaving police baffled as to the identity of her killer. The victim's name was Mary Pelham, also known within certain circles as 'Brighton Mary'. She lived alone on Portsea's notorious Blossom Alley and worked as a flower seller, amongst other alleged occupations. She'd been strangled before being bludgeoned to death with a bottle.

A neighbour, Ms Smith, described how she'd called at Ms Pelham's house, number 14, on Saturday, 27 January, and found her lifeless, chemise-clad body in bed. A blue scarf had been tied tightly around her neck and she was lying in a pool of her own blood. Ms Smith had last seen her neighbour alive at 11.00 pm the previous night. No sound had been heard coming from the house, despite the walls between the properties being extremely thin.

Though Ms Pelham was described as a private woman who never had any quarrels with anyone, there was a rumour about town that an unknown fair-haired sailor, who was seen entering her house on Friday evening, had recently threatened the flower seller with violence.

Over the coming months, the police probed each and every line of inquiry they came across. No expense was spared; several large-scale identity parades, involving an unprecedented 3,500 men, took place, but nobody was able to identify the fair-haired sailor.

The case took an interesting turn in the autumn of 1923, when the chief constable of Portsmouth received a message from a British warship in the Mediterranean that one of their sailors had committed suicide by throwing himself overboard. Two months earlier, the man had confessed to his shipmates that he was responsible for murdering Ms Pelham. Nobody took the claim seriously, as everyone assumed that the sailor was simply making a bad joke, but his suicide raised suspicion. The chief constable took the matter directly to Scotland Yard, but it was concluded that the alleged confession was of no importance, for the sailor was surely suffering from insanity at the time.

The mystery of who murdered Mary Pelham remains unsolved to this day.

The Sleepwalking Sailor

One night in about 1894, as reported by *The Northern Daily Mail*, the captain of a ship was awoken from his slumber when his first mate walked calmly into his cabin dressed in nothing but his nightshirt. Without a word, the mate picked up a jug of water from the captain's desk and proceeded to sprinkle the contents around the room, drenching his superior officer as he did so. It soon became clear to the captain that the mate was fast asleep; and when he'd completed his bizarre ritual, he returned the empty vessel to its proper place, departed the room and went back to his hammock without explanation.

The following morning, the mate had quite a tale to tell. He excitedly recounted to his shipmates how he'd woken during the night and had seen a ghost wandering around the room. Alarmed, he rose from his bunk and followed the spectre into the captain's cabin, where he proceeded to sprinkle the ungodly being with holy water. Satisfied that the cabin had been thoroughly exorcized, and that the captain was safe from the demonic influence of the netherworld, he returned to his bed.

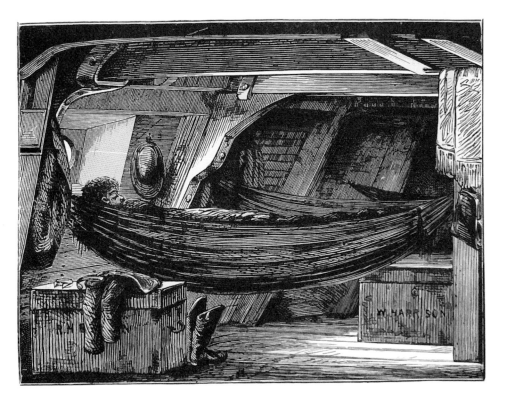

♪ The Dream Ship ♪

Eugene Field

Printed in *The Newcastle Courant*, 5 October 1895

When the world is fast asleep,
Along the midnight skies –
As though it were a wandering cloud –
The ghostly Dream-Ship flies.

An angel stands at the Dream-Ship's helm,
An angel stands at the prow,
And an angel stands at the Dream-Ship's side
With a rue-wreath on her brow.

The other angels, silver-crowned,
Pilot and helmsman are,
And the angel with the wreath of rue
Tosseth the dreams afar.

The dreams they fall on rich and poor,
They fall on young and old;
And some are dreams of poverty,
And some are dreams of gold.

And some are dreams that thrill with joy,
And some that melt to tears,
Some are dreams of the dawn of love,
And some of the old dead years.

On rich and poor alike they fall,
Alike on young and old,
Bringing to slumbering earth their joys
And sorrows manifold.

The friendless youth in them shall do
The deeds of mighty men,
And drooping age shall feel the grace
Of buoyant youth again.

The king shall be a beggarman –
The pauper be a king –
In that revenge or recompense
The Dream-Ship dreams do bring.

So ever downward float the dreams
That are for all and me,
And there is never a mortal man
Can solve that mystery.

But ever onward in its course
Along the haunted skies –
As though it were a cloud astray –
The ghostly Dream-Ship flies.

Two angels with their silver crowns
Pilot and helmsman are,
And an angel with a wreath of rue
Tosseth the dreams afar.

Mystery of the Mariner's Compass

One fine day in 1886, an American pleasure cruiser was sailing across Lake Ontario towards Niagara Falls. The party of people on board were in high spirits, eager to catch a glimpse of the spectacular scenery that awaited them. The captain was an experienced sailor, and was keen to impress his passengers with his smooth and competent navigation; but whenever his vessel came within sight of land, she always seemed to be 7 miles off course. He tried everything he could think of to follow the route correctly, but for some reason he couldn't seem to get it right, and found it impossible to reach his destination.

Greatly troubled, he began to doubt his skills as a mariner, for his navigational equipment all appeared to be in good working order. He surveyed his surroundings meticulously but could see nothing that would have interfered

with his compass. Just as he was gazing at the instrument, wondering what on earth he was doing wrong, the needle gave a sudden lurch. He looked up and noticed that a stout-looking fellow was walking across the deck. Inexplicably, the needle followed his movements, and when the gentleman reached the bow of the ship, the compass stopped and pointed directly at him.

Perplexed, the captain approached the passenger and enquired as to whether he was carrying anything magnetic upon his person. The gentleman insisted he wasn't, and to prove it he emptied his pockets, removing anything that was vaguely metallic. Even then the compass continued to follow him about the ship wherever he went.

The captain couldn't account for the extraordinary behaviour of his usually trustworthy instrument, until the portly passenger admitted that he'd been drinking nothing but iron tonics for the past few weeks, and suspected that his body must have become permeated with the metal.

The gentleman was referred to the Philosophical Society for further study, and began taking a spoonful of magnetic loadstones three times a day in the hope of removing the iron from his system. In the meantime, he was barred from going aboard any other vessel until his peculiar symptom had ceased.

The Churchwarden's Account

There's been a church in the North Yorkshire village of Alne since Saxon times. Dedicated to St Mary, the church has kept extensive parish records since at least the 1560s, and their churchwardens' accounts date back to 1696. These accounts, compiled each Eastertime, were records of payments made by the churchwardens throughout the year for such things as communion wine; linen washing; repairs to the church fabric; and the services of local artisans and labourers: plumbers, carpenters, stonemasons and even dog whippers, employed to chase away any unwelcome waifs and strays. Alne's accounts also include interesting footnotes in the form of a running social commentary, discussing the state of the parish and the country in general.

The churchwarden's entry for the year 1779 read:

This year England was in the greatest danger of an Invasion. The combined Fleets of France & Spain to the Number of 66 Ships of the Line appeared before Plymouth & We who had only 37 Ships & had for ages been reckon'd the first maritime Power in the World, were forced to resign the Dominion of the Sea to our Enemies. *O Tempora! O Mores!*

The Kentish Gazette published several articles that year reporting on these intended invasion attempts. 'The French are making preparations for an invasion upon England,' the paper explained. 'A placard has also been published at Paris, which is to be distributed throughout England, in case a descent takes place, setting forth that no violence will be used towards those of the British subjects who shall not appear in arms, or commit any hostilities.'

Needless to say, the British fighting spirit was strong. On 28 June, *The Hampshire Chronicle* explained how the inhabitants of Portsmouth and neighbouring districts applied for permission from the government to form a makeshift battalion to defend their shores against the French and Spaniards. 'As soon as they are furnished with arms and accoutrements,' the journalist wrote, '[the inhabitants] are determined to allot certain hours every day to learn the manual exercise.'

As it happened, their efforts were uncalled for. Alne's churchwarden concluded his account by explaining the reason why England was saved from invasion that year. 'Nevertheless by the Blessing of God, they did not land owing to an Epidemical Distemper wch rag'd among their Soldiers & Sailors.'

♪ Duncan at Camperdown ♪

William Cox Bennett
Published in *Songs for Sailors*, 1872

Come, sing of a name that is dear to renown;
Come, sing of our Duncan who won Camperdown;
You may talk of your Frenchmen, your Spaniards, and such,
But, for good honest fighting, now give me the Dutch.
If the roar of real broadsides you're longing to hear,
You've only to lay you alongside Mynheer;
That we've precious well known without any mistake,
Since Van Tromp and De Ruyter fought days through with Blake;
Your Mounseers and Dons fire above, not below,
They'd cripple your yards that away they may go;
But your Dutchman he fairly gets gun up to gun,
And batters your hull till he's lost or he's won;
And that's why with Nelson's we match the renown
Duncan won from De Winter at famed Camperdown.

From June to October we'd boxed it about
Off the Texel; but no, still they wouldn't come out
For gales none the tighter, for stores at a loss,
To Yarmouth we couldn't help running across;
There, while in the Roads we were victualling fast,
De Winter took courage and slipped out at last;
When, over the sands, the *Black Joke* signalled this,
It was all helter skelter the Dutch not to miss.
By noon we were out, with each stitch of sail spread,
Bowling onward due east with a sharp look ahead.
We'd been mutineering, but all that was done;
We'd got all we asked, and were sharp set for fun.
We'd sixteen good liners to win us renown,
And we sailed under Duncan who won Camperdown.

The eleventh at seven, at last all was right;
Trollope signalled 'To leeward, the Dutch are in sight.'
Then we pulled us together and just before nine,

There they showed, on the starboard tack, all close in line.
Twenty-one ships and four brigs were there sure enough,
And we knew we'd to deal with the right fighting stuff;
We knew there'd be sport before Dutchmen would strike,
We'd the day all before us, and work that we like;
We were all in a crowd, but 'twas pleasant to know
We couldn't go wrong if we went at the foe.
Up ran Duncan's signal: 'Close action', it flew,
And we cheered, for what that meant we very well knew;
We knew we went in to win fame and renown
For England and Duncan at famed Camperdown.

'Twas something the roar of their broadsides to hear
As we and our van ships closed up with their rear;
Through their line drove the *Monarch*, five minutes ahead,
The starboard ships leading, the larboard we led.
For De Winter we made, but before that we got
At him, their States-General would have it hot.
With what we gave to her she soon was content;
She sheered off and then at the *Vryheid* we went;
Then we found what they were as we fought gun to gun,
Little thought had our Dutchmen to strike or to run.
When their *Mars* and their *Brutus* and *Leyden* pressed round,
Quite enough to amuse us, I swear, men, we found.
It cost us, boys, something to win us renown
And a Peerage for Duncan at famed Camperdown.

Of the fun we were something beginning to tire
When the *Ardent* and *Triumph* took off half their fire;
And we didn't object when the *Powerful* came,
Greedy, with us, to take a full share of the game;
Mauled and bloody from fight in the midst of their four,
Hauling off, on the starboard tack, round then we wore;
But a broadside to give them we still could afford,
And down came their Admiral's masts by the board.
Riddled through and with all her three masts shot away,
With her starboard guns fouled, all disabled she lay;
With no bark or bite left her, the *Vryheid* might sulk;
What more could she do – a mere log of a hulk?

She was ours and she struck, but she shared our renown,
For she fought as we fought when we won Camperdown.

When De Winter gave in, they threw up the game quite;
When his colours came down, they had done with the fight;
We'd fought through thick weather, but, now we had won,
It cleared, just to let us see what we had done.
Now the drizzle was gone, we could count up our luck;
For nine of their line and two frigates had struck;
Their van ships, right in with the land, were in view;
But, in nine fathom water, what more could we do?
'Twas well to make sure of the prizes we'd got;
For they and we too had our full share of shot.
Before nightfall 'twas best to be well off the shore,
So we towed off our Dutchmen, full sail, for the Nore;
And you'll say 'twas a day that might well give renown
To us and to Duncan who won Camperdown.

Extraordinary Messages in Bottles

For centuries sailors on board doomed ships have sealed SOS messages, along with farewell notes to their loved ones, inside empty bottles and cast them overboard, in the vain hope that someday, someone, somewhere in the world, would discover them.

One such bottle was found in February 1929 on the beach of a northern Norwegian island, but it hadn't come from a seafaring vessel. This shell-encrusted champagne bottle had seemingly originated from a flying machine named *L'Oiseau Blanc*, piloted by the daring French airman, Captain Charles Nungesser. He and his mechanic, François Coli, had set off from Paris in a blaze of camera flashes on 8 May 1927, as they courageously attempted to fly directly to New York, a feat that had never before been achieved. The two airmen, however, were never heard from again.

The message inside the champagne bottle was written in English, and though the words were difficult to decipher, it apparently read:

Fallen into sea, May 4–5, 75 miles S Cape Farwell, Bell Isle. Rudder crushed, left wing broken. Both alive, but frozen stiff, and prepared for worst. 99 1-63. Coli.

Experts scrupulously examined the document, but it was never conclusively determined if it was genuine or, as many believed, simply a hoax. Whether the note was authentic or not, neither the airmen's bodies nor any evidence of wreckage were ever found, and the disappearance of *The White Bird* remains one of the greatest unsolved mysteries in the history of aviation.

In 1901, an American named Dr Carl A. Johnson was sailing across the Atlantic when, out of pure curiosity, he decided to drop his own bottle into the sea. Inside he'd sealed his contact details and a request that the finder, wherever they were in the world, should return it to him.

The finder turned out to be a young lady from Birmingham, who came across the bottle six years later on the coast of Rhyl, where she was holidaying. She entered into regular correspondence with the doctor and eventually they became engaged. By November 1910, their wedding had been booked, and Dr Johnson travelled to Birmingham to meet his bride for the first time. They spent their honeymoon by the beach at Rhyl, the place where their romance began.

In December 1914, a message of hope was recovered from a wine bottle on the beach at Brighton, and this one had come from a British warship of the First World War. It read:

To him or her who finds this bottle. – Six men of the light car section are fighting at the front, from which they all hope to return to dear old England in the near future. This bottle was cast into the sea at 9 p.m., 13-12-14.

Six soldiers signed the note: Walter Wakefield and Richard Hughes from Manchester; William Chapman and George Malin from Birmingham; Charles Bateman from Weymouth; and Harry Corres from Leeds.

A much more disturbing and sinister message was found inside a bottle that was floating down the river Thames. It was fished out in July 1921 and handed straight to detectives at Scotland Yard. The alleged writer was a homeless woman named Amy Marden, who claimed that three men had attacked her early one morning, knocking her unconscious. She ended the message with the words: 'I am now forcibly detained in the upper storey of a building near

Battersea Bridge. Help!' Though an investigation was launched, it was never reported whether or not the woman was found.

In February 1880, HMS *Atalanta*, a British training ship for young seamen, vanished without a trace. She'd been heading from Portsmouth to the West Indies, and on 31 January, departed Bermuda to begin her voyage home. She was never heard from again.

This mysterious disappearance drew attention to the lack of sophisticated methods of communication between ships in distress and the land. A sealed bottle, however useful it sometimes proved, was deemed inadequate, prompting an inventor from Portsmouth named Julius Vanderbergh to unveil his so-called 'Sea Messenger'. This was a small, sealed boat to which a bright flag, visible for a considerable distance, could be lashed. Each messenger was capable of carrying up to 60lbs of freight; hence a quantity of jewels or other valuables could be contained inside in the hope of being returned to loved ones back home. A passenger list, together with remarks on the cause of the disaster, and printed instructions in seven languages for the edification of the finders, was also enclosed before the messenger was committed to the deep. Though well intended, the invention never caught on.

Medicine Bottles at Sea

It was standard practice during the nineteenth century to issue sea captains with a medicine chest containing numbered bottles, should a member of their crew fall ill. They were also given a handbook, which explained the type of medicine in each bottle. Number seven, for instance, may have been the cure for bronchitis, and number three, a remedy for toothache.

One day, during a voyage in the 1890s, a sea captain was approached by a crew member who was feeling decidedly under the weather. After consulting the handbook, the captain concluded that a dose of number seven was required. However, when he went to his medicine chest, he found that bottle seven was empty. Thinking on his feet, the captain mixed a quantity of number three with number four, and dosed the suffering mariner with his homemade concoction, believing that just as the numbers added up to seven, so too would bronchitis be treated by mixing the cure for toothache with the remedy for scurvy. According to Blackburn's *Weekly Standard and Express*, printed on 23 May 1896, the captain couldn't understand why he later found the fellow 'dead as a hammer'.

♪ The Sailor's Dirge ♪

Printed in *Family Magazine*, 1880

Thy ship, they say,
Is in the bay,
And thou not of her number;
Beneath some far
And foreign star
They've left our boy to slumber.

No sweet friend keeps
Thy grave and weeps
By stealth where thou art lying;
But o'er thy home,
The white sea-foam
For evermore is flying,
But o'er thy home,
The white sea-foam
For evermore is flying.

The sea-moss spread
Is all thy bed,
The seaweed is thy willow;
The salt wave all
Thy shroud and pall,
The coral stone thy pillow.

Yet rest thee well,
The deep seashell,
Shall sigh with those that love thee;
And wild winds urge
From ev'ry surge
A solemn dirge above thee,
And wild winds urge
From ev'ry surge,
A solemn dirge above thee.

What did they do with the Drunken Sailors?

On the night of Monday, 9 February 1903, anyone passing Notre Dame Church at La Rochelle, France, would have been surprised to see – and hear – a drunken sailor, sitting astride the weathercock, singing at the top of his lungs. Even in his inebriated state, he'd somehow managed to climb all the way up to the summit of the enormous spire and perch himself at the pinnacle for several hair-raising moments. When the weathercock began bending under his weight, he shimmied down to the ground again, using the lightning conductor to aid his descent, and was promptly arrested. After he expressed his sincere regret, the magistrate took pity on him, and he was only fined 25 francs.

Unfortunately for the authorities, this wasn't an isolated incident. In April 1865, for instance, an inebriated mariner named James Smith was hauled before the Thames Police Court, charged with 'being drunk and disorderly, and with wilfully and maliciously doing spoil, damage, and injury to 1,200 eggs, against the peace of our Sovereign Lady the Queen, her Crown and dignity'.

The Herts, Guardian, Agricultural Record and General Advertiser told the whole sorry tale in their 15 April edition. An egg merchant named Ann Magner, who worked on the infamous Ratcliffe Highway, in the East End of London, claimed that the prisoner was so drunk that he fell against her window as he passed by. The glass broke, and all the eggs were smashed as they rolled out on to the pavement. However, Mrs Magner wasn't too unhappy, for it could have been worse: there were only 1,200 eggs on display that day, whereas she usually crammed up to 12,000 eggs into her window. The sailor was ordered to pay for the window and the 1,200 eggs, but he refused to accept the charge, claiming he hadn't acted deliberately. He disappeared shortly after receiving his wage at the shipping office, and Mrs Magner never heard from him again.

On another occasion, a sailor, who'd just returned to land, had spent the night of 22 September 1885 making merry in the taverns of Sunderland. He was so intoxicated at the end of his binge that he had no idea where he was. Thinking he was back at home, he settled himself down on the pavement of Low Street, by the river Wear, and proceeded to undress for bed. He removed all of his clothes and fell fast asleep, awaking hours later not only to discover the awkwardness of his very public situation, but also to find that his clothes had been stolen.

A rather more serious incident occurred in the summer of 1862, as a drunken seaman travelled on the Great Northern Railway. Deciding to have a bit of fun, he hauled out of the train window and scrambled on to the carriage roof, where he began to dance and frolic around. His fun was brought to an end when the train passed under a tunnel and the sailor was decapitated.

The Great Escape of Balmaceda

José Balmaceda was appointed President of Chile in 1886, and quickly introduced a series of much needed public and social reforms. He built schools, fortified the country's naval and military forces and constructed a network of public railways. Whilst the move was welcomed initially, the project soon became rife with corruption: building contracts weren't always awarded to the most deserving tenderers, and the work carried out was generally cheap and substandard. The president's popularity soon began to wane, and in 1891, after he'd tried to push an illegal budget through congress, the country descended into civil war. The vice president took control of the navy and an Act of Deposition was signed.

President Balmaceda was determined not to relinquish control without a fight, but his forces were defeated in battle and he fled, seeking asylum wherever he could find it. While the new provisional government searched the monasteries of Santiago for the fugitive, and troops guarded the snowy passages of the Andes Mountains, Balmaceda chose to hide in plain sight. He found refuge in the bustling seaport of Valparaíso, where he threw himself at the mercy of an American officer, Admiral George Brown, whose flagship USS *San Francisco* was anchored in Chilean waters. The ex-president pleaded for the officer to grant him the protection of the Stars and Stripes, for he feared what his enemies might do to him if he were caught. Admiral Brown agreed to help Balmaceda escape out of the country on board his ship, which was due to set sail for California. But how was this to be done? Balmaceda was probably the most recognisable man in Chile, so smuggling him on to an American vessel without being seen was not going to be an easy feat.

Eventually a cunning plan was devised: the admiral arranged for a disguise to be sent to Balmaceda's hideaway, and after donning his new attire, the fugitive waited for the cover of darkness before slipping out into a shadowy backstreet and heading for the harbour. The docks were crowded with men who would have relished the opportunity to seize the country's most wanted man and hand him over to the authorities – or else take the law into their own hands – but no one suspected a thing, for Balmaceda had assumed the role of a remarkably convincing drunken American sailor. Staggering along the wayside, his cap angled jauntily over his face, he made his way up the gangplank of the waiting vessel, becoming so absorbed in his character that he even performed a final drunken stumble, falling face first on to the deck. Once he was safely on board the *San Francisco*, he was given a private cabin, and remained out of sight for the entirety of the voyage.

By 15 September 1891, international newspapers were abuzz with the news that Chile's most wanted man had evaded capture, aided by an American admiral, no less. The news did little to ease political tensions between the two nations, but in the end it made little difference, for Balmaceda, still living in fear of retribution, shot and killed himself four days later.

♪ The Two Gunners ♪

Frederick E. Weatherly
Printed in *Family Magazine*, 1894

They sailed away, two gunners gay,
All in the summer weather;
They never had known one day alone,
Since they were boys together.
And now they go to fight the foe,
Across the stormy ocean,
With life in hand for Queen and land,
In faithful free devotion.

'Good-bye to the mountains and heather,
Good-bye, sweet home, good-bye!
We'll serve our guns together,
And at our guns we'll die!'

The fight was hot with shell and shot,
The foe had broke his tether;
And side by side the two old mates
Still served their guns together.
Right sharp all day they blazed away,
With gun to gun replying.
Till side by side they dropt and died
Beneath the colours flying.

Good-bye to the mountains and heather,
Good-bye, sweet home, good-bye!
They have served their guns together,
And at their guns they die!

Bravery at Sea in the Second World War

On 4 September 1940, *The Western Morning News* announced that the Victoria Cross had been posthumously awarded to a brave seaman who, despite being fatally wounded, carried on fighting in battle.

It was 4 July earlier that year, and the Second World War was in full force. HMS *Foylebank* was anchored at Portland Harbour, on the south coast of England, when enemy aircraft began firing on the ship. Acting Leading Seaman Jack Foreman Mantle raced to the starboard pom-pom gun and began to defend the ship, but his left leg was shattered by a bomb. He continued his duty nonetheless, standing fast and firing at the aircraft. The ship's electricity supply soon became damaged, so Leading Seaman Mantle had no choice but to abandon the pom-pom and resort to a hand-held weapon. As bombs and bullets continued to rain down around him, the sailor received one injury after another, but still he refused to abandon his mission and continued fighting until he fell.

Twenty-two bombs hit *Foylebank* during that frightful campaign, and as she was swallowed up by the waves, she took with her the lives of 176 crewmen.

The Western Morning News went on to describe the events that led to two fishermen being awarded the Distinguished Service Medal by King George VI. In 1940, Fred Barter, of Emsworth, in Hampshire, and Frank Lunn, of Fareham, were honoured for their extraordinary services during the evacuation of Dunkirk. They'd volunteered to serve their country at the outbreak of war, and in May 1940, during Operation Dynamo, the pair set out in a rowing boat to the shore of Dunkirk, with the intention of picking up as many survivors of the British Expeditionary Force as possible. Though their boat was only designed to hold six passengers, the fishermen succeeded in packing eighty fleeing soldiers into their craft, whilst at the same time towing a small raft containing a further twenty.

Just as they began their journey back towards their waiting vessel, a well-aimed enemy bullet put a hole in the side of the rowing boat, and all the men fell into the sea. Most of them made it back safely to the beach, but the two fishermen, determined to succeed in their mission, began swimming in the opposite direction. They battled against the open waves for more than a mile until they reached their ship, where they secured another rowing boat and returned to Dunkirk to try again. Eventually, after several dramatic trips, the two brave fishermen saved the lives of 400 soldiers that day.

Though the rescue mission was complete, the ship's commander, Captain H. Sparkes, sailed up and down the coast of France in the hope of finding more survivors. They stopped at a place called Fécamp, about 160 miles south-west of Dunkirk, where the two fishermen went ashore and called into a public house to ask if there were any English soldiers in the vicinity. They were met with stony silence, and soon realized that the place was full of Germans. Returning to the ship post-haste, the search was called off and the 400 grateful survivors were returned to their homes in England.

Seabird Omens

Different species of bird have, for many centuries, been considered omens of impending fortune or doom, bringing good or bad luck to whoever was fortunate – or unfortunate – enough to spot them. A white pigeon flying around a house, for example, was thought to foretell a marriage or betrothal of one of the occupants, whilst a flock of crows was a warning to landlubbers that death was near.

This wasn't just a terrestrial tradition: sailors and fishermen have long believed that seabirds bring their own particular signs and forewarnings. In 1926, a guillemot alerted the crew of an East Anglian fishing trawler that they were headed for misfortune. The bird had followed the trawler for some considerable time, and as the sailors believed that guillemots were harbingers of disaster, they weren't at all surprised when a storm began to brew and their vessel was wrecked in the middle of the North Sea. Fortunately for them, they were all rescued by another ship, and lived to tell the tale.

Gulls were generally regarded as good omens, especially by fishermen, for if a flock of gulls was spotted flying low over the sea, it was a certain indication that a shoal of fish was nearby.

The cormorant, on the other hand, was one of the most feared seabirds. According to the Biblical legend, Satan took the form of a cormorant and perched on top of the Tree of Life in order to spy on Adam and Even in the Garden of Eden, and a general distrust of the bird endured ever since. The *Evening Despatch* described how on 19 January 1940, during the Second World War, a cormorant was seen flying over HMS *Grenville* just before an enemy mine blew her to kingdom come.

In Scotland, a certain type of gull, known locally as a 'burl', was a warning against going to sea, as its appearance indicated that a storm was about to break. An old Scottish saying in fishing communities went: 'When you hear the burl cry, let you the boatie lie; two ebbs and a flood, let the weather be never so good.' Even when the weather was fair, if a burl was heard to emit a long, shuddering wail, a period of bad weather usually followed a few hours later; thus fishermen tended to heed the old rhyme, waiting twenty-four hours or so before taking their boats out to sea.

Another omen of bad weather was a bird known as the stormy petrel, so called because it was generally spotted during a downpour. The real reason for its appearance during a storm, however, was not to warn sailors of imminent trouble, but to feast upon the tasty crustaceans that were washed to the surface by tempestuous waves.

The albatross is perhaps the most sacrosanct seabird in maritime folklore. Seafarers have long held that when a comrade is drowned at sea, he is reincarnated as an albatross, and he returns to the ocean in his feathery form to guide others safely across the dangers of the deep.

♪ Left on Shore ♪

Sarah Doudney
Printed in *Family Magazine*, 1887

I would not be a culver
To coo the whole day long,
Till leafy woods in summer-time
Are weary of her song.

I would not be a field-lark
That builds a lowly nest;
Nor would I be a nightingale
That sings while others rest.

Oh, wings that flash in sunlight,
And shine through foam and spray,
If they were mine I need not pine
Upon the shore to-day!

For I would be a sea-bird,
And follow fast and free
The bonny boat that cleaves the main,
And bears my love from me!

The Chorus of 11,000 Parrots

In the late nineteenth century there lived a man in New York who was possessed of a keen sense of adventure and loved nothing more than exploring the remotest regions of the earth. In about 1888, according to *The Dundee Courier and Argus*, he set sail around the coast of Central America, stopping here and there to explore the wilderness with a party of comrades. During their expedition they adopted a tame parrot, and though it spent its days in the treetops of the surrounding forests, it would return to the ship each night in search of food and hearty company. Together the crewmen spent many merry evenings teaching the bird to sing a repertoire of popular shanties, as well as a selection of nautical expressions.

One day, happening upon an uncharted tropical forest, the explorers anchored their vessel and ventured into the heart of the jungle. After journeying for 28 miles or so, they stopped to make camp for the night. It was then they heard a familiar voice in the sky.

'Avast there, yo, heave, ho!' it squawked.

It was the parrot. It circled around the men's heads before settling down on a tree stump; then, with a shrill call, it summoned thousands of its feathered kin from all over the forest. All in all, the sailors estimated the presence of 11,000 birds. They fluttered around the ship's pet, settling in the treetops, vines and bushes that surrounded the campsite. Silence fell upon the jungle, until suddenly the tame bird burst into song.

> Of all the wives as e'er you know,
> Yeo ho! lads, ho! yeo ho! yeo ho!
> There's none like Nancy Lee, I trow,
> Yeo ho! lads, ho! yeo ho!

To the astonishment of the crew, all the other birds began joining in, just as if the adopted parrot had spent the past few months 'teaching' the lyrics to all its avian acquaintances.

The Captain and the Ship's Cat

For centuries it has been customary for seafarers to adopt a cat, which would help to get rid of any rats that happened to sneak aboard their ships. Though the arrangement was mostly practical, every so often sailors would become attached to their feline friends, and some even risked their lives to ensure the safety of their four-legged companions.

In November 1891, a ship called the *Advance* was wrecked at the mouth of the Tyne River. The lifeboats were launched, and Captain Osbourne, after having ordered his crew to abandon ship, remained on board until he was certain that everyone was safe. Just as he stepped into the lifeboat himself, he heard a sailor remark that the ship's cat was still in the cabin. Though the vessel was almost completely submerged, the valiant captain leapt out of the lifeboat and went straight below deck, without a thought for his own welfare. After a brief struggle he managed to break his way into the cabin, which was fast filling with water. He found his pet alive and well, and as he re-entered the lifeboat, his soggy moggy tucked safely under his arm, he brushed the perspiration from his brow and calmly announced: 'Now, lads, I think we're all here. You may shove off.'

♪ To Sea! ♪

William Cox Bennett
Published in *Songs for Sailors*, 1872

Through our veins the Norse blood courses;
No! not for the land are we;
The spirit of our fathers' forces
Their sons still to roam the sea.
For the salts of the ocean surges
Through our billowy pulses flow;
We must drive where the tempest urges
The sons of the sea to go
Wherever the wild winds blow.

Our land's but a rock of ocean,
Its storm's in our island breath;
In our lives is its restless motion;
We must out, though to wreck or death.
To our ears come the tempest's voices;
Our spirits those sea-tongues know;
Shore or wave? with the gale our choice is
From the land's dull life to go
Wherever the wild winds blow.

The Shipwrecked Dog

In March 1906, as reported in the *Aberdeen Journal*, a French fishing schooner, the *Hirondelle*, was wrecked in the Pentland Firth at the very northerly point of Scotland. The ship began sinking quickly, and Captain Coubel remained behind to see that all his crew escaped. There were no lifeboats on board; the ship was simply equipped with a 'rocket' life-saving apparatus: a device similar to a harness that travelled across a zip line, carrying one man at a time from the foundering vessel to the shore.

It happened that the captain had brought with him his beloved dog. Desperate to save the life of his four-legged companion, the captain draped his hound over the shoulders of the final crew member to leave the doomed *Hirondelle*, and watched as the duo zipped through the air above the turbulent waves.

Though the sailor and the canine reached the shores of Scrabster safely, the dog, upon realizing that his master was not among the rescued men, leapt into the stormy sea and began swimming back towards the ship; but before the faithful hound could reach the wreckage, the captain had already set off for shore along the zip line.

Captain Coubel was inconsolable when he landed and learned that his pet was missing but refused to believe his friend had died, for no body washed up. It was concluded that the dog must have turned around in an attempt to return to the landing point, but was swept further down the coast. If this was the case then he probably came ashore somewhere nearby. A thorough search was conducted, but there was no sign of the hound, and the shipwrecked sailors returned home to France without learning the fate of their crewmate.

The captain, however, never gave up hope of being reunited with his cherished *chien*. His prayers were answered some weeks later when news of the dog's whereabouts reached Calais. He'd been found alive and well, and had been adopted by a local man who refused to relinquish possession until he'd received £1 compensation for the canine's keep. The money was handed over at once, and a kind local lady, who was due to travel to the south of France, agreed to take the dog with her. On arrival at Calais, she was met by Mrs Coubel and the couple's children, as the captain had been taken ill with grief and pneumonia, and was too weak to leave his bed. The family and dog were overjoyed to be reunited, and the captain soon returned to full health. He vowed never to leave his companion's side again.

Monkeying Around at Sea

Victorian sailors were often known to take some kind of pet, such as a parrot or a cat, on their voyages; and in 1875, the seamen of HMS *Euryalus* adopted a large black monkey with a long tail. Though most of the crewmen were fond of their furry shipmate, the master distrusted it. For some reason, he became convinced that the creature was plotting to do something dastardly to the chronometer, so the master kept his navigational timepiece under lock and key at all times.

One day, however, the door to his cabin was accidentally left ajar, and the monkey seized his opportunity; he crept into the room and carried off the chronometer, just as the master had feared. The little thief rushed up the rigging as the master gave chase, tears clearly visible in his frantic eyes. He ordered his men to follow the monkey up the rigging, but however high they scrambled, the monkey climbed higher. As soon as the sailors were within an inch of the creature, he raised the chronometer over his hairy head, stretched his arms as high as he could, and flung the instrument into the sea, never for it to be seen again.

Another Victorian pet monkey who sailed on one of Her Majesty's ships accidentally fell overboard one day. A storm was raging and the sea was so high that the captain deemed it too dangerous to launch a lifeboat, but his crewmen protested so strongly that he finally relented. A plucky team of sailors rowed round and round in vain, looking everywhere for their lost friend, but no sight of him was had. With much sorrow they abandoned their mission and turned the boat around. Just as they reached the side of their ship, they spotted their pet, safe and dry. He'd climbed up the chain of the rudder and was sitting happily on the figurehead, grinning at his shipmates as if to mock them for their needless effort.

One of the navy's pet monkeys was a notorious character called Jocko. His human shipmates used to spoil him rotten, but when they also adopted a white kitten the monkey became exceedingly jealous. One day, as the little kitten was sleeping in the ship's netting, Jocko crept around to where his love rival lay. In a cruel act of vengeance, he stretched out his hand and tossed the helpless little creature overboard before anyone could intervene.

'Jocko was an abominable beast,' said one of the sailors during an interview with *The Chelmsford Chronicle*, printed on 3 December 1875. 'I could not bear him; he used to get drunk and play underhand tricks.'

It seemed, however, that Jocko was not all bad. Following the loss of their kitten, the ship's company adopted a spaniel, who gave birth to a litter of puppies during a voyage. Jocko was a curious creature, and was keen to take a closer look at the latest additions to his nautical family, but the new mother refused to tolerate the mischievous monkey. She guarded her pups fiercely, never allowing any of them out of her sight whenever Jocko was around. One day, however, she left her brood alone for the briefest moment, and returned to find Jocko sitting in her den, cradling the puppies gently in his arms. So tender and affectionate was he that from that day on the spaniel became more trustful of the monkey, and would even leave her offspring in the loving care of her newfound nursemaid while she went for her daily walkies round the ship.

♪ Sea Song ♪

Air – *Homeward Bound*
Printed in *The Shetland Times*, 23 March 1878

Hurrah! my boys, unfurl each sail
To catch the fair and freshening gale,
A nobler ship ne'er woo'd the breeze,
Nor sped across the bounding seas,
To the shores of Hobson's Bay.

A joyous crew are we, and gay,
As ever tasted the salt-sea spray;
Our hearts are true, and our arms are strong,
And Care never comes for he does not like our song,
And we're bound to Hobson's Bay.

Old England's hills are fading blue,
Farewell to Julia, Marianne, and Sue,
Farewell to publicans and two-pen'orths small,
To crimps, and policemen, and land sharks all,
For we're bound to Hobson's Bay.

I hear the voice of the rising blast,
The night-wind whistling around the mast,
I hear the petrel's doleful cry
Which tells that the tempest is drawing nigh,
While we're bound to Hobson's Bay.

But the wind may blow, our ship is strong
And steady the hand that steers her along;
We fear not tempest, nor rock, nor sand,
For Heaven is our protector and the captain has command,
And we're bound to Hobson's Bay.

And when we arrive at that distant shore,
Where dark mines yield the bright golden ore,
The song we will raise, and the wine-cup drain,

To the friends we have left beyond the wide main,
To sail for Hobson's Bay.

Now here is wishing joy to my own native shore
And the girl that I love, though I never see her more;
Success to the brave, and honour to the true;
And here, my jolly shipmates, a hearty health to you,
And the shores of Hobson's Bay.

The Sea-Lamb

The SS *Nereus* was a Greek cargo ship that was built in 1913 and wrecked in August 1937 off Cape Beale, Vancouver. Two years before the disaster, however, her master, Captain Elias Fonaris, found himself embroiled in an unpleasant legal case: he was hauled before a West Ham magistrate accused of breaking the strict Animals (Importation) Order of 1930 and the Disease of Animals Act of 1894.

In 1935, the ship came to port in Buenos Ayres, Argentina, where Captain Fonaris found an orphaned lamb. It so happened that foot and mouth disease was raging across the country, and the authorities were doing little to contain the outbreak, so the kind-hearted captain adopted the creature. He and his crew took it on board their ship and allowed it to travel with them across the world, but were careful never to let it set foot on dry land.

The lamb wasn't the only animal on board: the captain also had a cow, which provided his crew with fresh milk. One day, as the ship journeyed from South America to England, the cow kicked the lamb overboard. The distraught captain ordered the helmsman to turn the ship around, and after a frantic two-hour search of the shark-infested waters, the lamb was eventually rescued. It was alive but greatly exhausted, and it took the crew three days to nurse the poor thing back to health.

When the *Nereus* eventually arrived at London the lamb was discovered, and Captain Fonaris was summoned to appear before a magistrate, Mr St John Morrow, accused of bringing a potentially infected creature into the country. Extensive measures had hitherto been taken in Britain and across the Colonies in an attempt to eradicate foot and mouth disease, and it was clear, according to the prosecutor, Mr G.F. Thompson, that the defendant had acted in an indefensibly reckless manner. He argued that instead of taking pity on the lamb, Captain Fonaris should have ordered the animal's destruction, and recommended that it be disposed of without delay.

The captain pleaded guilty, expressing his sincere regret for any wrongdoing, but stressed that he'd only acted out of mercy. He pleaded for the magistrate to allow him to return the lamb to Buenos Ayres, rather than have it killed. His crew stood by him, and together they agreed to indemnify him against any fine that the court chose to levy on him.

It seemed that the magistrate was a fellow animal lover, for he dismissed the case under the First Offenders' Act; both the captain and the lamb were exonerated.

Bear on Board

The *Marchesa* was a schooner that set sail from Cowes, on the Isle of Wight, on 8 January 1882, bound for the Far East. Anyone observing her from a distance could have been forgiven for thinking she was an ordinary ship, just like any other, but if they dared to venture on board they would have been sure of a big surprise: one of her crew members was an enormous bear named Misky.

Though this unlikely mariner tolerated his shipmates reasonably well, he didn't take too kindly to strangers. This was a fact that a newly recruited lieutenant learned all too well when he stepped on board one day, wearing his navy jacket and bicorn. The bear, perhaps attracted by the strangeness of the officer's uniform, started bounding across the deck towards the uninvited visitor. The sailors' cries of 'Don't worry, sir: it's only his fun!' did little to reassure the quaking lieutenant, and were no comfort at all when the lolloping beast seized the officer by his coat tails, pulling him into a suffocating bear hug. He only managed to wriggle free by slipping himself out of his jacket, which the bear carried away triumphantly.

One morning, a sailor caught the smell of burning in the air. He followed the aroma into the galley, where he found Misky standing one-legged on top of a red-hot stove. With his front paws he was reaching for a shelf above his head, trying to pinch a handful of cabbages. When the stove became too hot for him, he'd switch legs, but otherwise seemed oblivious to the fact that his paws had become red raw.

As the bear grew older, his antics grew wilder, until he became almost uncontrollable. He finally crossed the proverbial line when he ate a portion of the cabin skylight, which he washed down with a sailor's finger. That was when the captain finally realized he could no longer keep his pet, and Misky was sent to a retirement home in London's Zoological Gardens.

♪ The Wave ♪

L. Blanchard

Printed in *The Bradford Observer*, 30 December 1841

My being I take from fountains that break
In the depths of the ocean sand,
And my form is curl'd through the liquid world,
To freshen the green dry land.
And the drops I fling from my watery wing
As it mounts to meet the day,
Are gems for the hair of the sea girls fair,
That rise on my shining way.

I glide with a smile o'er the coral pile,
By the ocean snake entwin'd,
And sweep in my track the whale's broad back
With the scattered foam behind,
Then I sing for hours to leaves and flowers
That never beheld the moon,
But sprinkle their sheen of gold and green,
To thank my lingering tune.

The white could on high (the wave of the sky)
I choose for my shadowy bride,
And she comes sometimes from her shoreless climes,
And kisses my conscious tide,
But like all that's fair in earth or air,
She dissolves in silent pain,
And weeps on my flood her silv'ry blood,
That gushes in sparkling rain.

The Power of a Whale's Tail

In about 1887, an engineer from Glasgow named John Henderson conducted a study into the amount of energy generated from a single blow of a whale's tail, and calculated it to be equal to 145 horsepower when the whale was swimming at the rate of 12mph. In other words, the amount of energy generated was the equivalent of around 106.6kW. In today's world, that amount of electricity would probably be sufficient to boil about sixty kettles.

Mr Henderson's calculations were based on an 80-foot-long fin whale weighing 74 tons. The width of its tail was about 20ft. These enormous creatures, surpassed in size only by the blue whale, were sometimes spotted in British waters during the nineteenth century, though no Victorian inventor ever succeeded in devising a method of harnessing the immense power of their tails.

Killer Octopus

It wasn't uncommon for nineteenth-century fishermen to encounter octopuses during their excursions, and some could even return home to tell their families that they'd been grabbed around their arm or leg by a slimy tentacle or two. Few, however, had ever been harmed – or worse, killed – by a mollusc. That was until the autumn of 1883, when a 14-year-old boy was fishing at Tomioka, on the Pacific coast of Japan. Without warning, a gigantic octopus stretched out two of its tentacles from the water and seized the young lad tightly, dragging him into the ocean. The boy's cries alerted some nearby men, who, after a brief struggle, were able to cut him loose. They rushed him back to his home, but he later died from his injuries. It was thought that the octopus must have been of a venomous variety, though the exact species was never identified.

♪ How we got our India Ink ♪

J.S. Goodwin
Printed in *The Leicester Chronicle & Leicestershire Mercury*, 18 June 1887

In a low down cave of the torrid India sea
Dwelt a cuttle fish old and grey,
The sea moss hung on his back in a fold,
And his arms were a sight to appall the bold;
And his eye shot a baleful ray,
Just think!
And his eye shot a baleful ray.

On a coral crag of an iridescent reef,
Where the ambergris jeweled the waves,
Lived a beautiful maid of the *mer* régime,
As supple and smooth as an anchorite's dream,
And she never lured men to their graves,
Not she!
She never lured men to their graves.

Now the old grey squid from his cellar submarine
Caught a glimpse of the mermaid white;
And his heart beat fast with an amorous thud
As he leered from his den in the oozing mud;
And he said, 'I will have her this night,'
The brute!
He said, 'I will have her this night.'

And so when the beams of the silver-gilded moon
Came down for the maiden's play,
The cuttle fish squirmed from his nest in the slime,
And with horrid arms knotted began to climb
Toward the home of the sea-nymph gay,
Oh, shame!
Toward the home of the sea-nymph gay.

But the Neptune bold of the trident-pointed spear
Has an eye on his subjects weak;

49

As the monster crawled and hugged the rock,
A streak, and a flash, and a blinding shock
Put a stop to his little freak,
How nice!
Put a stop to his little freak.

For, warned by the words of the hoary-headed god,
The maiden had time to think.
She called from his seaweed bed her steed,
And with sword of fish she caused to bleed
From that squid, his India ink.
That's how
We got our India ink.

Devoured by Sharks

In the spring of 1910, the SS *Oceana*, which had set sail from New York towards Bermuda, lost four of her men during the voyage.

Not long after the vessel departed, a stoker appeared to become unhinged and threw himself overboard for no apparent reason. The captain immediately ordered a lifeboat to be sent out after him. Six men climbed into the boat and duly went to search for their lost comrade; but during the frantic dash to lower the lifeboat into the sea it crashed into the side of the ship and was broken up, hurling its occupants into the water. Only three of them were rescued. The others were left to the mercy of the man-eating sharks that were spotted bobbing up and down in the waves.

The British Navy's Pet Shark

Over the years there have been uncountable instances of people keeping unlikely pets. The great painter Rembrandt had a pet ape; the politician Sir John Lubbock kept a wasp as his companion, and a nineteenth-century lady from New York once adopted a boa constrictor so it could 'befriend' her infant niece.

Perhaps one of the most curious pets of all was a shark named Old Tom, who lived in the waters of Port Royal, Jamaica, during the late eighteenth century. He was reputed to have been 20ft long, and was adopted by senior officers in the Royal Navy to prevent sailors from deserting the men-of-war ships. Tempted by the juicy pieces of bullock's liver that were throw into the ocean for him, Old Tom used to circle the warships, striking fear into the hearts of any man who may have been thinking of jumping overboard and swimming to shore. In fact, so well cared for was Old Tom that sailors were often heard complaining that the shark received better rewards than they did.

The navy learned that sharks didn't make good pets when Old Tom gobbled up a young lad who worked for the island's sugar traders. All that was recovered was the boy's undigested watch.

♪ Trafalgar ♪

Tune – *The Bay of Biscay*
William Cox Bennett
Published in *Songs for Sailors*, 1872

North-west the wind was blowing,
Our good ships running free;
Seven leagues lay Cape Trafalgar
Away upon our lee.
'Twas then, as broke the morning,
The Frenchmen we descried;
East away, there they lay,
That day that Nelson died.

That was a sight to see, boys,
On which that morning shone!
We counted three-and-thirty,
Mounseer and stately Don;
And plain their great three-deckers
Amongst them we descried –
'Safe,' we said, 'for Spithead,'
That day that Nelson died.

Then Nelson spoke to Hardy,
Upon his face the smile,
The very look he wore when
We beat them at the Nile!
'We must have twenty, Hardy,'
'Twas thus the hero cried;
And we had twenty, lad,
That day that Nelson died.

Up went his latest signal;
Ay, well, my boys, he knew,
That not a man among us
But would his duty do!
And as the signal flew, boys,

With shouts each crew replied;
How we cheered as we neared
The foe, when Nelson died!

We led the weather column,
But Collingwood, ahead,
A mile from all, the lee line
Right through the Frenchmen led;
'And what would Nelson give to
Be here with us!' he cried,
As he bore through their roar
That day that Nelson died.

Well, on the *Victory* stood, boys,
With every sail full spread;
And as we neared them slowly,
There was but little said.
There were thoughts of home amongst us,
And as their line we eyed,
Here and there perhaps a prayer,
That day that Nelson died.

A gun – the *Bucentaure* first
Began with us the game;
Another – then their broadsides
From all sides through us came.
With men fast falling round us,
While not a gun replied,
With sails rent, on we went,
That day that Nelson died.

'Steer for their admiral's flag, boys!'
But where it flew none knew;
'Then make for that four-decker,'
Said Nelson, 'men, she'll do!'
So at their *Trinidada*
To get we straightway tried,
As we broke through their smoke,
That day that Nelson died.

'Twas where they clustered thickest
That through their line we broke,
And to their *Bucentaure* first
Our thundering broadside spoke,
We shaved her; – as our shot, boys,
Crashed through her shattered side,
She could feel how to heel,
That day that Nelson died.

Into the Dons' four-decker
Our larboard broadsides pour,
Though all we well could spare her
Went to the *Bucentaure*.
Locked to another Frenchman,
Our starboard fire we plied,
Gun to gun till we won,
That day that Nelson died.

Redoubtable they called her –
A curse upon her name!
'Twas from her tops the bullet
That killed our hero came,
As from the deck, with Hardy,
The bloody fight he eyed,
And could hear cheer on cheer,
As they struck, that day he died.

'They've done for me at last, friend!'
'Twas thus they heard him say,
'But I die as I would die, boys,
Upon this glorious day;
I've done my duty, Hardy,'
He cried, and still he cried –
As below, sad and slow,
We bore him as he died.

On wounded and on dying
The cockpit's lamp shone dim;
But many a groan we heard, lads,

Less for themselves than him:
And many a one among them,
Had given, and scarcely sighed,
A limb to save him
Who there in glory died.

As slowly life ebbed from him,
His thoughts were still the same;
'How many have we now, boys?'
Still faint and fainter came.
As ship on ship struck to us,
His glazing eyes with pride,
As it seemed, flashed and gleamed,
As he knew he conquering died.

We beat them – how, you know, boys,
Yet many an eye was dim;
And when we talked of triumph,
We only thought of him.
And still, though fifty years, boys,
Have gone, who, without pride,
Names his name – tells his fame –
Who at Trafalgar died?

Shark Papers of the Caribbean

In 1799, a naval scandal sent shockwaves through the British West Indies: an American brig, the *Nancy*, was suspected of smuggling enemy goods! These were the days when four sparring countries filled Caribbean waters with friction and suspicion. Britain, Spain, France and the Netherlands were engaged in a bitter colonization campaign, each vying to be masters of the sea. Though America was neutral, it came as a bitter blow for Britain when they found evidence suggesting that their brothers across the Atlantic were trading with the Dutch.

Fingers immediately pointed towards the *Nancy*, which had set sail from Baltimore to the Dutch island of Curaçao on 3 July that year. From there she journeyed to Haiti, where a British ship, HMS *Sparrow*, was sent to intercept her. After a fleeting chase, she was captured and escorted to Port Royal, Jamaica, where a thorough search of the vessel commenced and all of her cargo seized. *Nancy's* captain, Thomas Briggs, was questioned at length, but, to Britain's surprise, nothing incriminating was found. To all intents and purposes, everything was legitimate, and it appeared as though British suspicions were unfounded. A furious Captain Briggs even produced official documents that cleared the ship of any wrongdoing.

Just when it seemed that the Americans were about to be acquitted, Fate dealt Britain a surprising hand. A lieutenant named Michael Fitton, of the Royal Navy, was cruising off Port Royal on board HMS *Ferret* when he caught a shark. Inside the creature's stomach was a bundle of papers, which, it transpired, were the *Nancy's* real documents, proving beyond any shadow of a doubt that the vessel was indeed carrying contrabands of war. Captain Briggs had thrown these official papers overboard when he realized the *Sparrow* was on his tail, and a passing shark had devoured them. The papers he'd handed

over to the British were fakes. A further search of the *Nancy* was conducted, and secret hideaways containing the concealed commodities were discovered.

The shark's jawbones were inscribed with the words 'Lieut Fitton recommends these jaws for a collar for neutrals to swear through', and were put on display at Port Royal before being sent to the Royal United Services Institution in London. The papers remained in Kingston's Institute of Jamaica until 14 January 1907, when a catastrophic earthquake destroyed the building, along with many others in the city.

The Shark that Sparked a Murder Mystery

The Coogee Aquarium, which first opened in Sydney in 1887, was a popular tourist attraction during the late nineteenth and early twentieth centuries. Boasting a colourful aquarium, an indoor swimming pool, a bandstand, donkey rides, and an open-air bar, there was always plenty of entertainment for visitors; but in 1935 the main attraction was a newly caught tiger shark. The public's curiosity turned to alarm when, on 25 April, the shark regurgitated a whole human arm. At first it was feared that the man-eating creature must have killed someone prior to its capture, but upon examination it was concluded that the man's arm had already been severed from the rest of the body before the shark had eaten it. This led the police to assume one thing: there'd been a murder!

The first piece of evidence was a length of rope that was found attached to the wrist of the arm, suggesting that the apparent victim had been restrained. The second clue, relating to the identity of the deceased, was a distinguishing tattoo. Investigations were launched at once, and the brother of a missing man was able to confirm that the tattooed arm belonged to his brother, 45-year-old James Smith, a small-time crook and former boxer who ran a local billiard saloon. The arm's fingerprints also matched Smith's. He'd been missing for several days, leading the authorities to conclude he'd been murdered and his body chopped up by a person or persons unknown before being dumped into the sea.

Three weeks' worth of intensive investigations ensued, until detectives finally received information from a local businessman and known criminal named Reginald Holmes. He alleged that on 9 April a convicted forger named Patrick Brady visited him. He turned up on Holmes's doorstep covered in blood and confessed to the murder of Smith. Brady proceeded to blackmail Holmes, threatening him with the same fate if he didn't pay him a considerable sum of money.

The three men had been involved in a huge insurance scam concerning a ship named *Pathfinder*, which was deliberately wrecked off the coast of New South Wales. The trio were due to pocket the insurance money, but before they could do so, there'd been a bitter quarrel. According to Holmes, Brady cut up Smith's body and placed it inside a tin trunk, before taking it out to sea and throwing it overboard.

Further intelligence revealed that on 8 April, the day Smith had disappeared, he'd told his wife he was going fishing. However, he was later seen in a hotel bar on the outskirts of Sydney, drinking, talking and playing cards with Brady. That was the last time Smith was seen alive.

Patrick Brady was duly arrested and charged with murder.

Another witness, an estate agent, soon came forward, claiming that he'd let one of his seafront cottages to Brady back in March. On 17 April, after the lease had expired, the agent went to inspect the cottage. At first glance it seemed that the property had been left in an immaculate condition, but it soon became clear that a few things were amiss: the rowing boat had been left in a sorry state and several household items were missing, including a rug, a rope, the boat's paddle and a tin trunk. A whole tin of kerosene had been used up, and for some reason a mattress had been replaced. Furthermore, traces of human blood were found. The police began to suspect that Smith had been murdered in the cottage.

Things were looking hopeful for the prosecution until Reginald Holmes was found dead in a motorcar on 12 June, hours before he was due to give his evidence in court. The vehicle was recovered from the lonely shadows beneath Sydney Harbour Bridge. Holmes had been shot three times in his chest, and with no star witness to testify, the case began to crumble.

Things went from bad to worse in the final week of June, when Brady successfully applied to the Supreme Court for a prohibition order on the grounds that a single arm didn't constitute a body. Without a body, there was no proof that a murder had even been committed; and with nothing but circumstantial evidence remaining, the case was dismissed. Brady walked free.

Perhaps the drinkers and diners who still visit the site of Coogee Aquarium – which reopened as a leisure complex, Coogee Pavilion, in 2014 – ever wonder what became of the rest of James Smith's body, which was never found.

♪ Grandfather ♪

F.E. Weatherly, MA
Printed in *Family Magazine*, 1875

Over the downs to the morning sea,
The children dart and run,
And grandfather watches them happily,
As he sits at the door in the sun.
'My blessings on their merry hearts!'
With trembling voice says he,
'They bring the prime of life's morning time
In the twilight back to me.'

Over the downs to the morning sea,
The children dart and run,
Waving their wee hands merrily
To grandfather there in the sun.
'What would they do were he to die,
And go from them far away?'
And they silent stand on the yellow sands,
And ponder amid their play.

Over the downs to the morning sea,
The children dart and run,
And grandfather's praying quietly,
As he sits at the door in the sun.
Play on, ye happy little ones!
Old grandfather, quietly pray!
Beyond the seas and the stars and suns,
Ye shall meet in heaven one day.

The Engineless Steamship

In 1880 it was announced that a German engineer named Dr Emil Fleischer had designed a remarkable new type of steamship, one that had no engines, screws, sails or paddles. It was launched at Kiel, in the north of the country, and was propelled by a type of apparatus known as a hydromotor, which forced jets of steam out into the water, thereby propelling the vessel forward.

The steam was generated by an ordinary ship's boiler, and passed through a series of pipes to the hydromotor, which contained an arrangement of valves, pressure cylinders and discharge nozzles. Under pressure, the steam was forced from the ship into the ocean with considerable velocity, causing the boat to shoot forward over the waves. All that was required of the captain was to simply turn a lever on the bridge, and the vessel would set off, maintaining an even course. There was scarcely any noise, save for the rushing of the steam from the tubes in the hydromotor; and the ship could be brought to a halt by the alternate use of the lever.

According to *The Northern Evening Mail*, naval authorities deemed this new ship 'as simple as it is effective', and hopes were high that the design would revolutionize navigation of the future. The newspaper went on to report that this vessel 'completely abolishes all risks from accidents to rudder or machinery, since there need be no rudder, and there is scarcely any machinery'.

The first vessel to be powered by a hydromotor was named *Pellworm*, after the German island. She was 75ft long by 12ft beam, and was capable of steaming 6 knots an hour, the equivalent of a little over 3mph.

Anti-Seasickness Ships

In the days before commercial aeroplanes could be seen in the sky, merchants and travellers relied on seafaring vessels to venture abroad. This was a pleasant undertaking for many, but for thousands of others their journeys were made almost unbearable by that debilitating ailment known as seasickness.

The engraving opposite illustrates a novel craft, dubbed the anti-seasickness ship, which was designed in about 1880 by a man named Edward Smith, from the industrial town of Bradford in the West Riding of Yorkshire. His invention was fundamentally a ship within a ship: movable fastenings, attached to the hull of the outer ship, V, were connected to a smaller inner vessel, *V*, which was floated on oil and held in position by a system of wheels and racks. It was this inner vessel that contained the saloon and cabins of the passengers (shown at A), and also plenty of space for cargo and storage (B). The idea was that as the ship was tossed and rolled by the waves, the floating chamber maintained its upright position, keeping the crew and passengers steady, even in the stormiest weather.

An American designed a similar invention: a berth that remained perfectly level and steady while at sea. This novel contrivance was found to be of service to individuals who suffered from seasickness, and even travellers who simply disliked the sensation of being tossed about during a night of rough weather. It operated on a gimbal basis, similar to the action of a compass needle, and consisted of an ordinary berth, which was hung and balanced in such a way for it to maintain its horizontal position during the voyage.

This revolutionary bed was successfully trialled on board a steamer named *City of Alexandria*, and testimonies of passengers who spent the night in one were glowing. It soon became evident that the anti-seasickness berth was more practical than Mr Smith's anti-seasickness ship, though neither idea

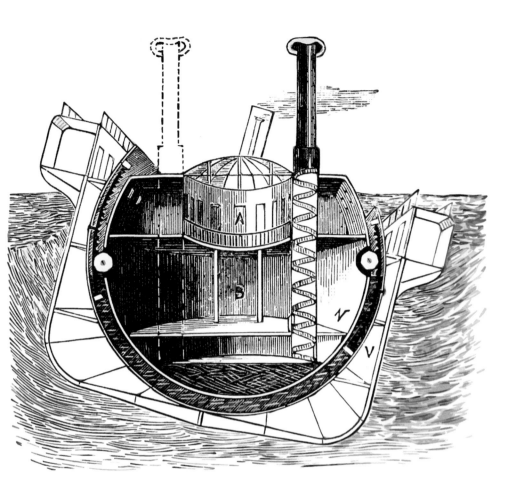

ever really caught on in the construction of modern passenger vessels. This may have been partly due to the catastrophe that befell the *City of Alexandria* in the winter of 1893. The ship exploded during a voyage from New York to Havana when a cargo of 400 puncheons of spirits caught fire. She and the self-levelling berths were entirely destroyed, and dozens of lives were lost.

♪ A Life on the Ocean Wave ♪

By a 'Bad Sailor'
Printed in the *Leicester Chronicle*, 27 June 1885

'A Life on the Ocean Wave!'
The man who wrote it was green;
He never has been at sea,
And a storm he never has seen.

He never has seen a wave
As it dashed o'er the vessel's deck;
He never has seen a fire at sea,
Or been floating upon a wreck.

He never has been aroused
From his morning's gentle doze
By the sound of the splashing water,
As it fell from the horrid hose.

He never has heard a man
Scrubbing right over his head,
With a noise sufficient to arouse
From the grave the slumbering dead.

He never has seen a fat woman
Growing thinner day by day,
And leaning over the vessel's side
Throwing herself away.

While people look carelessly on,
Though in tears the woman may be,
And unfeelingly say it is nothing at all –
Only the roll of the sea.

Seasick he never has been to his toes,
And crept into bed in his coat,

While every motion increased his throes,
And his feelings were all in his throat.

This man may have sailed in a boat
In some puddle or on a sound;
But if he has been to sea and wrote
Such a song he deserves to be drowned!

The First Ship Equipped with Electricity

The public's interest was sparked in the springtime of 1880 when it was announced that a new type of vessel had been completely equipped with modern electrical conveniences, making it the first commercial example of its kind. This was the steamship *Columbia*, built in Chester, Pennsylvania, for the Oregon Railway and Navigation Company. She was lit by Edison's electric light throughout the saloons and staterooms. There were 120 lamps in total, similar in appearance to traditional oil lamps, and were specially adapted so that in the event of an electrical breakdown, oil could be substituted so the crew and passengers would not be without light. The dynamos generating the electrical current were situated in the engine room and looked after by an electrical engineer; but the lights were controlled by a steward. He decided when to extinguish the lights in the saloons, so as to intimate the hour for retiring.

In addition to the electric light, all the rooms on board were fitted up with electric call-bells, and the smoking rooms were connected to the steward's cabin by telephone. The captain's cabin also had a telephone, allowing him to communicate with the steward, purser and engineer; and there was an electric device on the bridge that enabled him, by simply pressing a button, to obtain all the necessary information about the performance of the engine. Furthermore, the ship was equipped with state-of-the-art electrical elevators for loading and unloading her cargo; and the electric headlight at the front of the vessel was able to turn in any direction, projecting a powerful beam of light for several miles over the sea.

The *Columbia* soon began making regular trips between Portland and San Francisco, to the awe of her passengers, and others who read about her in the newspapers.

This successful introduction of electricity at sea soon prompted other shipping companies to follow suit, but disastrous events in 1907 served to demonstrate that even the most advanced technology can never be a match for the brutal forces of nature. It was midnight on Saturday, 20 July when the *Columbia* collided with the wooden freight steamer, *San Pedro*, off the coast of Shelter Cove, about 280 miles north of San Francisco. A terrible fog had descended across the region, and despite the ship's powerful electric headlight, the approaching freight steamer hadn't been visible until it was too late. Though the wooden *San Pedro* managed to stay afloat, *Columbia's* bow was sliced open. Sleeping passengers scarcely had any warning, and 150 people lost their lives that night, including every single female passenger on board. Captain Doran went down with his vessel, having refused to abandon ship.

The Russian Tsar's Floating Palace

In the late 1870s, the Russian emperor, Alexander II, commissioned a floating 'water palace' in the form of a new steam yacht named *Livadia*. She was designed by a Russian, Admiral Popov, and manufactured by a British shipbuilding company. Replacing an older version of the same name, which sank in 1878, this magnificent state-of-the-art vessel was completed in 1880 and launched from the Glaswegian shipyard of Messrs John Elder and Co, to the cheers of several thousand spectators who'd lined the banks of the river. At first, sceptics feared that the emperor was secretly building a deadly warship under the guise of a pleasure yacht, but these fears were soon laid to rest when the marvellous vessel was unveiled.

Besides being a masterpiece of shipbuilding art, the *Livadia* was also a scientific novelty. She was hailed 'the most remarkable vessel afloat' by the *Sunderland Daily Echo and Shipping Gazette*, and was effectively a 'floating palace' carried on the back of an enormous turbot-shaped raft. *The Birmingham Daily Post* went so far as to suggest, on 22 October 1880, that she could be 'likened to a small village with its 200 or 300 inhabitants', though only a dozen or so people were usually seen on board at any one time; the others may have been found dining in the palatial dining rooms, or smoking on the verandah that ran around the entire perimeter of the ship. Below this were lines of terraces containing whitewashed dwellings for the rich and famous passengers.

The emperor had a grand saloon resembling a country villa, which, according to the paper, occupied 'almost the whole of the fore part of the awning deck'. Its interior was a 'marvel of decorative art in the style of Louis Seize', containing a colonnade of Ionic pillars, electric candelabras, a marble fountain and large windows offering panoramic views of the passing scenery.

There was also plenty of open space on board, reserved for activities such as lawn tennis; and for pleasant summer evenings there was a glazed and cushioned summer house. The corridors were paved with marble, and at the centre of the vessel were the boiler and engine rooms, as well as luxurious bathrooms, extending from one end of the ship to the other. So sumptuous and exclusive was the yacht that a journalist for *The Star* newspaper, writing on 23 November 1880, stated that she was 'luxurious almost beyond the dreams of fairy tales'.

The engraving opposite represents the vessel during a voyage. The state saloon is shown in front of the bridge, with the imperial apartments beneath it on the second deck.

The lines of the turbot-shaped raft on which the palace stood swept round into a point at the bow and stern. The peculiarity of its shape was specially designed to obviate uncomfortable motion during a rough sea. The breadth at the widest part was 153ft, and the length was 235ft. At the stern was a downward projection, which held three propeller screws. There were nine boilers, three to each screw; the horsepower was 10,500, and the speed was up to 16 knots per hour. She was manned by 250 men, but was only provided with two lifeboats.

In September 1880, a month prior to the launch of the *Livadia*, word reached the shipyard that a group of Nihilists, hell-bent on causing carnage, were plotting to blow up the yacht. It was alleged that two Russians and one other individual of undisclosed nationality were planning on conceal pieces of highly explosive nitroglycerine among the coals that were used to stoke the engines, so the Glaswegian police were on high alert. Though the plot was ultimately foiled, a young Russian revolutionary named Ignacy Hryniewiecki succeeded in assassinating Tsar Alexander II on 13 March 1881, by throwing a bomb at his carriage as he travelled through St Petersburg.

Despite all the pomp and ceremony, a report in *The Portsmouth Evening News*, printed on 2 February 1883, suggested that the *Livadia* didn't live up to expectations. 'In particular,' the newspaper explained, 'it is complained that the machinery shakes the vessel so much that she is anything but the comfortable floating palace she was expected to be. It is believed that she will be broken up.'

Soon afterwards, all the onboard luxuries were removed and the ship was converted into a grim prison hulk, and renamed *Opyt*. In 1926, after forty-three years of detaining a variety of convicts awaiting deportation to a penal colony, the one-time floating palace was written off and sold as scrap metal.

♪ To Our Brothers in America Talking of War With Us ♪

William Cox Bennett
Published in *Songs for Sailors*, 1872

Yes, yes; we sent our armies forth
And dared to think war right, 'tis true;
But that was, brothers, 'gainst the North,
The despots' stay, not such as you;
Yet then we clung to peace, how long!
And almost truckled to the Czar,
And almost owned the right the wrong,
Rather than curse the world with war.

Now shall we play the despots' game?
Oh, let this senseless wrangling cease!
In blood, in rights, in tongue, the same,
We talk of war! Peace, madmen, peace!

Too much of war before to-day,
Of mutual hate and loss we've had
That losing game again to play;
Oh, brothers, no, we're not so mad.
Shoulder to shoulder, you and we,
Twin boasts of liberty should stand;
The strength, the vanguard of the free,
The help of every fettered land.

And shall we play the despots' game?
Oh, let this senseless wrangling cease!
In blood, in rights, in tongue, the same,
We talk of war! Peace, madmen, peace!

What would the tyrants of the earth,
From German Prince to Russian Czar,
Think you, think such a struggle worth,

Where Freedom slew herself with War?
How would they laugh! full sure of this,
When every deadly blow was dealt,
Whoe'er it struck it could not miss
To be too well by Freedom felt.

What! we – we play the despots' game?
Oh, let this senseless wrangling cease!
In blood, in rights, in tongue, the same,
We talk of war! Peace, madmen, peace!

O mighty freemen of the West!
O mightier, greater, yet to be!
He who from you for us would wrest
One right of yours, accursed be he!
You owe us much: how great your debt,
To you it need be told by none;
And cursed be they who would forget
The ties that make both nations one.

What! we – we play the despots' game?
Oh, let this senseless wrangling cease!
In blood, in rights, in tongue, the same,
We talk of war! Peace! madmen, peace!

Oh, shall mere trifles such as these,
For such a crime afford pretense?
To let this frenzy on us seize,
For such things, shows us void of sense.
No, leave them to some friend's award!
What if we lose? 'twere better far
Than if we won them with the sword –
The cursed wickedness of war.

We will not play the despots' game;
Oh, let this senseless wrangling cease!
In blood, in rights, in tongue, the same,
We talk of war! Peace, madmen, peace!

The Folding Pocket Boat

An ingenious new maritime invention, known as the folding boat, was described in *Bell's Weekly Messenger* on 10 September 1864. Its purpose was to assure the survival of all who sailed the seas; and its inventor, Captain Sayer, a magistrate from Kent, earned the praise of several public bodies including the Society of Arts and the Royal United Service Institution.

These folding boats were especially advantageous owing to their remarkable portability and buoyancy. The smallest model, which was claimed to be both storm-proof and unsinkable, measured 7ft long by 2ft 3in wide. Though it was large enough to carry two persons, it folded up into a light, compact bundle, small enough to be carried in one's pocket. The largest boat measured 26ft 6in long by 5ft 8in wide, and could comfortably seat forty-five people, perhaps slightly more in an emergency. When folded up, this model occupied less than 4in in space, making it an ideal piece of equipment for a sailor's sea bag.

By 1881, an American inventor had unveiled a similar vessel made of waterproof canvas. It measured 12ft in length, and could carry two passengers and 600lbs of cargo. These canoes came flat-packed in boxes about 38in cube, and could be assembled in two or three minutes.

The Telegraph in Arctic Travel

Since the time of the Ancient Greeks, daring pioneers have attempted to reach and explore the Arctic Circle. This was finally made possible during the nineteenth century, with the help of modern vessels and navigational tools. The North Pole, however, wasn't reached until the twentieth century, when, in the autumn of 1909, British newspapers heralded the news that the veteran Arctic explorer, Commander Robert Peary, of Pennsylvania, had become the first person in history to reach this elusive place. He symbolically nailed the Stars and Stripes to the spot on 6 April that year, although news of his highly contested achievement didn't reach the rest of the world for another five months. Perhaps if Commander Peary had adopted the use of the Arctic telegraph, devised twenty-eight years earlier, he could have relayed the news of his discovery to his ship as soon as he set foot on the Pole.

It was James Gamble, the general superintendent of the Western Union Telegraph Company at San Francisco, who suggested in 1881 that sledge parties chasing the Pole, or striking out across the ice for geographical purposes, ought to take with them a coil of telegraph wire, which they could lay out along the ice as they proceeded. Ice was known to be a good electrical insulator, so a bare steel wire weighing about 20lb per mile served the purpose, and as 100 miles of it would only weigh 2,000lbs, it wouldn't hamper the progress of the party. A battery on board the explorers' ship provided power for the line, and the sea acted as the return wire, provided the ice was bored through, and an earth contact for the wire was obtained in the water underneath. Upon receiving the telegraph message, the crew on board the ship could immediately send a dispatch vessel to deliver the news to an eager public waiting patiently back home. Furthermore, as well as being a handy communication device, the metal line doubled up as a guide for the explorers to follow on their return journey.

♪ A Thousand Leagues Away ♪

William Cox Bennett
Published in *Songs for Sailors*, 1872

The wind is blowing fresh, Kate, the boat rocks there for me;
One kiss and I'm away, Kate, for two long years to sea;
For two long years to think of you – dream of you night and day –
To long for you across the sea – a thousand leagues away,
A thousand leagues away, dear Kate,
A thousand leagues away;
While round the Pole we toss and roll,
A thousand leagues away.

I half could be a landsman, Kate, while those dear eyes I see,
To hear the gale rave by without, while you sat snug with me;
But I must hear the storm howl by, the salt breeze whistling play
Its weird sea-tune amongst the shrouds, a thousand leagues away,
A thousand leagues away, dear Kate,
A thousand leagues away;
While South we go, blow high, blow low,
A thousand leagues away.

I'm too rough for a landsman's lot – his tame life's not for me;
What could I do ashore for you? – my fortune's on the sea;
The mate of winds and billows still, I must my fate obey,
And chase the whale before the gale a thousand leagues away,
A thousand leagues away, dear Kate,
A thousand leagues away;
The blubber boil, and stow the oil,
A thousand leagues away.

Something I have, and more shall have, if luck my fortune be;
Enough at last a wife to keep, and children round my knee;
And do you love me well enough, Kate, from your heart to say,
'I'm yours, though you must win me, Will, a thousand leagues away,
A thousand leagues away, dear Will,
A thousand leagues away;

For you she'll wait; go, win your Kate,
A thousand leagues away.'

One kiss; the tide ebbs fast, love; I must no laggard be,
Upon the voyage I'll hope, love, will give a wife to me.
Pray for us, Kate; such prayers as yours God bids the winds obey;
By fortune heard, your loving word will speed us far away.
A thousand leagues away, my Kate,
A thousand leagues away;
God will befriend the lad you send
A thousand leagues away.

The Electrical Self-Steering Ship

Throughout the nineteenth century, a helmsman's task in rough weather was an arduous as well as a dangerous one, but in 1881, an engineer named W.F. King introduced a new apparatus, termed the 'self-steering compass', which promised to revolutionize marine navigation.

To demonstrate his invention, Mr King arranged for the helm of an oceanic liner to be operated by a hydraulic apparatus, powered by the electric current from a single voltaic cell. A compass, which had a metal-tipped index, was set to the course the ship was required to follow. If ever the ship diverted off-course, even by a degree, the metal point of the index came into contact with a pin, thus completing the circuit of the battery and turning on the hydraulic apparatus, which automatically moved the helm to port or starboard until

the true course was recovered. As soon as this happened, the compass needle moved, and the circuit was broken.

The accuracy of the steering was said to be even greater than that of the most experienced helmsman, but as no electrical apparatus was completely infallible, it was still considered necessary to have a human helmsman in reserve, just in case.

The Water Velocipede

In 1868, reports came flooding in from Paris regarding a new aquatic novelty that was being used by pleasure-seekers on Lake Enghien on the outskirts of the capital. It was dubbed 'the water velocipede', and was essentially a bicycle crossed with a boat. By 1882, Prince Albert, the Prince of Wales (later King Edward VII), had introduced this novel mode of transport into England, and he was regularly seen cruising in his own water velocipede at the seaside or on Virginia Water Lake at Windsor Castle.

The model shown in the illustration was designed by Captain Lundborg, a renowned naval engineer. It was made from two long boats that were connected together and bore a platform for the passengers' seats and pedals, which turned the two paddlewheels. When the sea was calm, speeds of up to 7 or 8mph could be realized.

♪ England ♪

William Cox Bennett
Published in *Songs for Sailors*, 1872

O England, awe of earth, how great art thou!
Mother of nations, filler of the lands
With freemen, free-born, who is like to thee,
Or hath been? Egypt and the vanish'd rules
Of Asia swept the earth, but desert winds
That blasted races, and, death dealt, were gone,
Their records, ruins. Greece arose and lit
The dark with glory, but a falling star,
How bright, how fleeting! save that yet her thoughts,
Less mortal than her Gods, illume us still.
Rome came and saw and conquered, crushed and pass'd
Smitten by freemen, she and all her slaves.
Gone are the thrones that the eternal sea
Heap'd riches on and empire – billows huge
That roll'd, and roar'd, and burst upon her shores,
Tyre and the pomp of Sidon – Afric's boast,
Swart Carthage – Venice, and the ocean rules
Of Genoa and of Holland – all are gone.
Spain is the mock of nations once who shook
Even at the utterance of her iron name.
These and their glories are but mutter'd dreams
That by the past's dead lips are feebly told;
But we endure, we, sceptred heirs of power,
Victory and empire, fated to endure,
Gathering fresh might and glory through all time.
Our glory is our safeguard. Wall'd we stand
With mighty memories – buckler'd with bright fames;
Our present, still 'tis pillar'd on a past
That lifts it, glistening in time's marvelling gaze,
An awe and wonder to the trembling world.
Yes; were we aged – did our great life die out –
Were England palsied, as the nations are
That once knew greatness, phantoms of the past
Would rule earth for us, and the subject seas,
So long our tributaries, at the thought
Of what we have been, still would crouch and cringe,

And fawn upon our footstool; but, thank God!
Greatly we stand on greatness – rock–like, plant
Feet adamantine through the flow of time,
No muscle loosening; ever widening still
Stretch the broad bases that uprear our strength,
And thrust us skywards; the hot vines of Spain
Ripen beneath our shadow; the green world
The barks of Palos bared to Europe's gaze,
That is our children's heritage; the isles
That chafe the tropic billows feel our tread;
Lo, other Englands gather in the south,
And 'neath the glare of India we tread out
The bloody wrath that writhes beneath our heel,
And shield the maddening nations from themselves.
Where is the earthly air that has not borne
The record of our glory? What far race
But, naming greatness, to its children tells
Foremost our triumphs, all the mighty names
That are our greatness? For what land on earth,
Sceptred or crownless, can bid glory count
Hero for hero with us – fame for fame?
Earth boasts one HOMER; we, one yet more high,
SHAKESPEARE. If Florence hush her soul in awe,
Naming her DANTE, hell, and heaven's sweet air
Were breathed by MILTON. Who to wisdom taught
How to be wisest? BACON. NEWTON lived,
And God's dread secrets straight man wondering read,
And all the worlds revolved in order'd law.
WATT made the might of Nature's primal powers
Our toiling bondslaves. DRAKE and wandering COOK,
PARRY and PARK and all their fellows trod
Billow and laud, and made them paths to man.
Look, knowledge lightens thought from land to land;
That did our WHEATSTONE. Fame, to name our great,
Were weary ere the flaming roll were told,
And still she writes, what glories! on the scroll,
Courage and wisdom kin to greatness gone,
Those that the blasting path to Lucknow trod,
And smote curst Delhi and its brood of hell,
HAVELOCK and LAWRENCE – names fit mates to those
Who broke the dusky ranks at Plassey first,
And far Assaye, and crush'd Ameer and Sikh

At Meeanee and red Ferozeshah,
And crowned our brows with empire. Crécy's fame,
And mailed Poitiers' and Agincourt's had heirs
In Blenheim and Corunna, and the fields
Of WELLINGTON – Vittoria and its peers,
And the wild, earth-felt shock of Waterloo.
O ye old sea-kings, to whom your tossed decks
Were thrones to rule the lands from, from you sprung,
In us lives on your scorn of all that pales
Weakness – in us your hunger of renown.
Sea-roamers – grapplers with the might of storm –
Stern tramplers of the billows, fitting sons
To you were DRAKE and HAWKINS, and the hearts
That with fierce joy, for God and right, went forth
And wrapped the Armada – the Invincible –
In their red wrath, and whelm'd it in the deep.
Brother to you was he whom our proud lips
Name proudly – BLAKE, who, many a bloody day,
Grappled with Dutch VAN TROMP, and thundered down
The broadsides of DE RUYTER. Kin to you,
O ye old Norse hearts, who dared look on death
And greet him loud if victory with him came,
Were later glories. From your fierce veins sprang
The fiery blood of ROOKE, who gave La Hogue
To glory – MONCK and SHOVELL – BENBOW – HAWKE –
DUNCAN of Camperdown – HOWE – RODNEY – he
Who at St Vincent thunder-calmed the winds –
And of him, mightiest, whose fierce voice of war
Nile and the Dane heard, crouching – he who gave
To us the ocean's rule at Trafalgar.
So triumph grows to triumph. From the fire
Of by-gone fames we light the glories up
That sun the present. Oh, should danger threat,
New vauntings front us, and the shock of war,
In the red smoke of battle shall we feel
The awful presence of our living dead,
Steeling our hearts to conquer. Hellas heard,
At Marathon, and Salamis, heard clear
The roar of Ares, and the hero shout
Of Ajax pouring flight amid her foe.
The stern dead DOUGLAS won at Otterbourne;
So WELLINGTON our charging ranks shall hurl

Through future triumphs; through all coming time
Shall foes' masts crash and struck flags flutter down,
We conquering in the thought we can but win
Whose blood is NELSON'S. Nor is fame alone
The bulwark of our greatness. Strong we stand
In surer strength that fates us not to fall;
For we have breathed the breath that knows not death,
Hers in whose might we dread not the decay
That palsies nations. At the mighty breast
Of Freedom were we nurtured. At her knee
Have we drunk in the mighty lore that gives
To nations immortality and youth
Eternal. To our hands she gave the spell
That masters monarchs. From her lips were caught
The charging cheer of Edgehill, and the shout
That at red Naseby scattered far her foes.
Strong in her strength, we strengthen – conquering
And still to conquer, while we do her will.
Us does she gift with wisdom. We are wise
In Courts and counsels – all that builds up States,
And from the clash of thought do we shock out
Fit light to walk by – truths, by which we walk
More and more wisely; but, O island home
Of freemen, thee a future beckons on,
Lit with a glory thou hast never known,
And great with greatness that for thee shall be.
Lo, thou hast walked in sunlight that is night
Seen by the radiance of that perfect day.

The Over-Sea Railway

Developed in the late 1800s, the Florida East Coast Railway runs for 351 miles along the eastern coast, connecting the northerly and southerly tips of the state. Though it was seen as a remarkable feat of nineteenth-century engineering, by 1905 technology had developed to such an extent that railway authorities began to ask, why terminate the line at Miami? It had recently been announced that the Panama Canal, a new waterway linking the Atlantic with the Pacific Ocean, was going to be constructed, and this inspired railroad engineers to concoct their own ambitious plans: they proposed to extend Florida's coastal railway more than a hundred miles over the sea, connecting the United States with Cuba.

It was fully expected that once the engineering work was completed it would be possible for a traveller to journey from the New England States all the way to Santiago de Cuba without even changing carriages. Though storms would rage across the Atlantic and the Gulf of Mexico, passengers could expect to ride in comfort on board luxurious Pullman carriages that would chug along the 127-mile over-sea extension. The track was to be built on top of gigantic viaducts that linked each of the coral islets known as the Florida Keys, before terminating at Key West. From there, the trains were to be shipped 90 miles to Havana, on board giant ferries.

Though the region's tempestuous weather had caused the shoals of the Florida Keys to become mottled with shipwrecks, the ocean waves never rose above 25ft, even in the fiercest storm; ergo the railroad was built 30ft above sea level. A thick concrete wall was constructed on either side of the embankment, further protecting the trains from the ferocious winds.

The longest stretch of ocean between the Keys was measured at 7 miles. To span this gap, a viaduct consisting of 120 arches was required. A total of 2,500 labourers were set to work to build it, and for this section of railroad they used 300,000 barrels of cement; 200,000 cubic yards of rock; 3,000,000 feet of timber; and 7,000 tons of reinforcing rods. The foundations of the viaduct were built on the seabed, 60ft below the surface of the waves. It wasn't much easier building over land, for certain parts of the islands were covered in swampland, which the railway had to cross. To make matters worse, in October 1910 Florida was hit by one of the worst hurricanes in history, and the extension work was greatly damaged. About 3 miles of track was blown away and a huge number of lives were lost.

Despite the obstacles, the work was a success, and Florida's over-sea railway finally opened for traffic in 1912, having been dubbed by the American media as one of the greatest engineering triumphs of the age. The first train to cross the ocean set off from Jacksonville at noon on Sunday, 21 January, arriving at Key West the following day. In honour of its arrival, the islanders threw a three-day long celebration.

The line was eventually closed on 2 September 1935, when a terrible storm, known as the Labor Day Hurricane, caused millions of dollars worth of damage. Instead of paying to have it rebuilt, it was reopened in 1938 as an over-sea highway, and still operates as such to this day.

The Whistling Buoy

Until about 1880, buoys anchored over sunken wrecks, or shoals, or other undersea obstacles were often difficult for mariners to distinguish during bad weather, and on a dark night they were practically indistinguishable. They proved so hazardous to seagoing vessels that a new type of buoy was conceived. It was known as the 'Courtenay Automatic Whistling Buoy', which, as its name suggests, emitted a deep, booming whistle, loud enough for masters of approaching vessels to discern.

It was the motion of the buoy that caused the sound: as it bobbed up and down on the waves the air inside it was forced through a whistle. Furthermore, each buoy could emit its own distinctive call, which was especially helpful when a number of buoys were moored in the same area. In fact, its inventors suggested that each buoy could be made to announce a distinctive letter or word, according to the Morse telegraphic alphabet of signals.

These whistling buoys weighed 15 tons each, and it was calculated that as they moved up and down on the waves, even during calm weather, a force of nearly three horsepower was created. The illustrious inventor, Thomas Edison, realized he could utilize this otherwise wasted energy to drive small electric generators that powered electric lamps, helping the buoys become even more discernible on dark and stormy nights.

Though naval authorities all agreed that these whistling buoys would be of great service, residents who lived within the range of the whistles voiced their objections strongly. However, it was the buoys' troublesome tendency of going adrift and getting lost in the middle of the ocean that ultimately led to their fall in popularity.

♪ My Son at Sea ♪

Charles Johns
Printed in *Family Magazine*, 1882

The moon is bright, the stars to-night
Shine in a cloudless sky;
The moonlit sea sleeps tranquilly
And on its gently heaving breast
The tired wind slumbers, lulled to rest
By Nature's lullaby, lullaby.

Shine on, O moon! Stars, clearly shine!
May the calm unbroken be!
God guard all souls who sail the brine!
God bless my son at sea!

Far, far away where night is day,
And austral billows swell
He sails my boy, my pride, my joy
Sails over day-lit southern seas
Comes from the fair antipodes
The son I love so well!

Sail on, good ship, while fond waves leap
About you joyously, joyously.
Lord, when I wake and when I sleep,
Guard Thou my son at sea!

The Lavish Lifebuoy

The sketch below, dated 1881, illustrates a new type of lifebuoy, invented by a sailor named Mr Whitby who worked on board HMS *Excellent*. Like ordinary buoys, it comprised a hollow ring, divided into airtight compartments, but it also came with a number of upgrades. Firstly, a long chain was attached to the bottom of the ring, so that a castaway sailor had something to stand on. Furthermore, by resting his back on the inside of the ring, the person had free use of his hands, so he could comfortably hail a ship by raising a flag up the attached pole, or by flashing lights or flares, all of which were provided. The buoy was so innovative, in fact, that it lit up automatically when it came in contact with water. For foggy weather, a whistle was included; and the buoy could be easily hoisted on board a passing vessel by lowering a line from the yardarm, thus avoiding the inconvenience of having to launch a lifeboat. Finally, it was claimed that the new design was less bulky, more buoyant and far cheaper than an ordinary buoy.

The Life-Saving Umbrella

The illustration of an umbrella, from 1881, shows an example of a combined lifebuoy and umbrella, which passengers who were unable to swim sometimes took with them on their voyages. On rainy days it was used just like an ordinary umbrella, but it transformed into a lifebuoy in the event of an emergency.

The inflated buoy is shown at A A. Light netting was sometimes added to the outside of the umbrella, allowing a person in distress to cling to it with ease.

♪ From a Distant Land ♪

M.C.G.

Printed in *Family Magazine*, 1882

She sat within the little room,
And heard the storm beat on the pane;
Within was loneliness and gloom,
Without was cold, and wind, and rain.

The fire had sunk within the grate,
The bird was songless in his cage,
And she, forlorn and desolate,
A weary woman bowed with age.

She sadly mused on all her woes –
The wind howled louder than before;
She heard a knock, and slowly rose,
And took a letter at the door.

O happy letter, bringing joy,
That trembled in her wrinkled hand!
For her beloved sailor boy
Had written from a distant land.

Sweet fancies filled her heart in crowds,
The bird began to warble sweet;
The sun came out through jagged clouds,
And made a shining in the street.

The dying fire blazed up anew;
She set the feeble lamp alight,
And laid her scanty meal for two:
'Who knows but he may come to-night?'

The Portable Bath for Travellers

In the 1860s, local and national newspapers up and down the country were peppered with advertisements for portable baths, made by a company named Cording. These, it was claimed, were perfect for travellers, for they could be taken aboard ships and used inside cabins.

The woodcut image below represents a portable bath from 1882. This model came with its own reservoir and water heater. The tank held enough water for a single bath, and the heating chamber adjoining the tank heated the water before it came out of the tap.

Though this new product was regarded as a remarkable invention, by the turn of the century cruise liners had started to afford their passengers the luxury of running water, so the necessity of portable baths soon began to diminish.

The Pneumatic Boat-Suit

The illustration below shows a kind of wearable, inflatable boat that was designed in America in the late nineteenth century. It was unveiled in Britain in about 1895, intended for use by swimmers, sailors and travellers.

It consisted of a rubber shell resembling a horse collar, with waterproof leggings and boots attached, forming the bottom part of the vessel. The swimmer simply inserted his legs into the waterproof leggings and drew the boat up to his waist. Using a tube, he inflated the pneumatic collar before entering the water.

The sailor could either propel the boat through the water using his hands and feet, or by hoisting a small sail and allowing the wind to guide him across the waves. Though a handful of fishermen tested the vessel, a lack of space for their hauls was perhaps the reason why the invention never became too popular.

♪ My Johnny ♪

Printed in *Family Magazine*, 1884

My Johnny is a sailor,
And a-sailing he would go.
I said, 'Oh, Johnny-lad, take me,'
But Johnny-lad said, 'No.'

So I stayed with the childer,
And the childer stayed with me;
There's little Sal, she's just turned five,
And Molly's nearly three;
And Johnny went aboard his ship,
And sailed away to sea.
I cried, 'Dear lad, come quickly home,
Come quickly home to me.'

The winter passed so slowly,
The summer came so sweet;
I watched and watched for Johnny,
And longed again to meet.

And still and still I'm watching –
I'm watching by the sea;
And little Sal and Molly, too,
They stand and watch by me;
And when we see him coming,
A happy day 'twill be –
The happiest, oh! the happiest
There e'er can dawn for me.

The Sea-Swimming Suit

The year 1875 brought good news for those who sailed the oceans, for it was announced that a new sea-swimming suit had been designed, which promised to make drowning a thing of the past. It was the invention of an American engineer named C.S. Merrirnan, and was introduced to Britain by the renowned Irish swimmer, Captain Paul Boyton.

The rubber suit was simple in design, being made in two parts that were joined at the waist. It consisted of an inner and an outer skin; the space

between the two was divided into air chambers. Once the wearer had donned the suit, he simply inflated the chambers by blowing into a tube, and he was ready to go.

The ensemble came with a paddle, which, in favourable wind, doubled up as a small wooden mast and sail. A watertight trunk was also attached, in which up to ten days' worth of food and provisions could be kept. For added convenience, it was pre-packed with a small lamp, a number of signal lights, a long knife and an axe.

Though reports of castaways' lives being saved by this imaginative garment were few and far between, Captain Boyton made the headlines when he crossed the English Channel wearing Merrirnan's sea-swimming suit. With food, brandy, cigars and other provisions safely packed in the floating trunk, he set off from Dover at 3.20 am on 10 April 1875. The suit not only kept him afloat, it also protected him against the icy temperature of the water. The double-ended paddle propelled him along at a good speed, but he was forced to abandon his attempt after about fifteen hours.

His second attempt, on 28 May, was a success. He set off from Cape Grisnez in France at 3.00 am, finally walking ashore at Fan Bay, near Dover, twenty-three hours and thirty minutes later.

The Sea-Swimming Machine

By 1880, a new piece of seafaring technology had been patented and unveiled, which was expected to be of particular service to sailors in the Royal Navy, as well as athletes, tourists, hobbyist swimmers and 'amphibious enthusiasts'. It was dubbed 'the novel swimming machine', and was invented in the 1870s by an American named Dr Richardson, of Mobile, Alabama.

Prior to its launch, tests in the Gulf of Mexico had all proved successful, and the inventor had high hopes that his new machine would become an essential nautical commodity. In fact, as reported in *The Bury Free Press* on 24 January 1880, Dr Richardson claimed that his invention could 'render it possible for a tourist on a fine summer day to cross from Dover to Calais by his own muscular efforts with as little difficulty, or, at any rate, with as much certainty, as he can go from London to Dover on a bicycle'.

The contraption comprised a cork float and waterproof dress, which were attached to a screw propeller by a long, thin shaft. Two cranks were fastened to the shaft, one at the top and the other at the bottom, just above the propeller. To operate the machine, the swimmer would lie flat on the float and operate the cranks with his hands and feet, in the same sort of manner as riding a bicycle. The cranks turned the propeller, which thrust the machine forward in the water.

Dr Richardson claimed that a swimmer could expect to reach speeds of up to 5mph, meaning that it could have taken an aquanaut setting off from Dover a little more than four hours to reach the shores of France.

♪ Beachy Head ♪

G. Weatherly
Printed in *Family Magazine*, 1890

Like some grim giant who has dared to fight
And conquer two stern foes – Time and Decay,
Rugged and scarred through ages passed away,
Its huge cliffs rise in bold majestic height,
In storm or sunshine gleaming ever white;
And, strong in knowledge of security,
It even dares to laugh to scorn the sea
That lashes it at times with angry might.

O guardian beacon of our British coast,
Live on, live on, as in the bygone past,
Fit type to us (whate'er the threat'ning host)
Of England's glory, hard to overcast,
Of England's strength – no infant of an hour,
But giant-statured, giant-like in power.

Walking on Water

Since Biblical times, the ability to walk on water has only ever been bestowed upon the most blessed individuals, and they were few and far between. By 1880, however, it seemed that the gift was finally within the reach of the rest of the populous. It was announced in *The Manchester Courier* on 13 August that an inventor from New York, Mr Soule, had designed a pair of shoes that granted the wearer the ability to cross a stretch of water 'with as much facility as on dry land'. The shoes were 5ft long, and on the soles were five moveable boards that opened and closed depending on the movement of the walker. The paper claimed that the shoes were so effective that Mr Soule was able to cross a body of water 'without any difficulty, through the crowd of steamers, sailing vessels, and barges'. He was said to have resembled a skater gliding gracefully across a frozen lake.

Later, on 15 October 1898, the *Yorkshire Telegraph & Star* declared that a German mariner, Captain Grossmann, had also invented a pair of shoes that allowed individuals to perform the same feat. His patented device was basically a pair of tin tubes, pointed at each end, which were worn by the water-walker like ordinary shoes.

The design was adapted and modified over the years, and in February 1907 national papers were full of the sensational news that an American seaman named Captain Charles Oldrieve had achieved a hitherto impossible feat: he'd walked all the way from Cincinnati, Ohio, to New Orleans, Louisiana, over the course of forty days, and every single step had been on water. Using a pair of specially adapted wooden shoes, each measuring just over 4ft long, the captain completed his 1,600-mile journey down the Ohio and Mississippi rivers. Setting off on New Year's Day, he accomplished his watery meander on 10 February without the aid of any kind of vessel, although he was accompanied by Mrs Oldrieve who travelled beside him in a rowing boat. His achievement won him a place in the record books, as well as $5,000 from some associates who'd wagered that he'd never succeed.

In March that year, Captain Oldrieve publically announced that his next mission was to walk across the English Channel, from Dover to Calais, and after that, the Atlantic Ocean; but he was destined never to attempt either challenge. Following the accidental death of his beloved wife, who was burned to death at a firework display, the captain committed suicide by ingesting a lethal quantity of chloroform. He died on 12 July 1907, five days after his wife's decease.

How to Drink Seawater

In 1880, the French Navy revealed that they'd adopted the use of a 'distilling machine', which turned seawater into pure, drinkable water. The machine, invented by a naval engineer named Mr Perroy, was divided into three parts: the first contained an aerator; the second, a refrigerator; and the third, a charcoal filter. A quantity of seawater was heated up, and the resulting steam passed through the aerator, which condensed the steam into water. After then passing through the refrigerator and filter, a fresh supply of drinking water was produced.

♪ Three Answers from the Sea ♪

From *Family Magazine*, 1880

'Sea! sea! sea!
What will you bring for me?'
'I'll bring you sands, smooth stones, and shells;
Lilliput rivers and tiny wells;
Wonderful seaweeds strange and wild,
To please your fancy, my pretty child.'

'Sea! sea! sea!
What will you bring to me?'
'Star-lighted glances by moonlit waters;
Dreams of Eden for Eve's fair daughters;
Morning sunshine, sweet evening's shade
To bless and gladden thee, gentle maid.'

'Sea! sea! sea!
What canst thou bring to me?
I am a toiler like thy waves,
And worn and wasted like thy caves;
Oh, so weary! I dare not think –
For I seem to stand on the crumbling brink
Of that wide ocean without a shore,
Into which I must plunge for evermore.'

'Weary toiler, I bring thee a breath
From the Ocean of Life. Lo! the Shadow of Death
Is blown to the winds like a broken cloud.
Hark to my waves! they laugh aloud
With merry ripple and jubilant roar,
As they rush to efface thy cares once more.

'Rest! rest! rest!
Fling thyself down on thy mother's breast;
Touch the earth, like the Titan of old,
And arise with strength renewed and bold;
Draw a deep breath of my pure sweet air
And thy heart shall expand to do and dare –
Yes – to do and dare thy highest and best
Till the calmer ocean brings perfect rest.'

The Course Indicator

The novel course indicator, shown in the accompanying diagrams, was introduced to seafaring vessels by 1892. It was a simple yet ingenious new design for headlamps, which intended to reduce the number of collisions at sea by indicating the direction in which the ship was travelling.

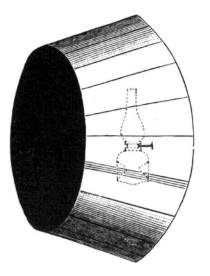

The indicator, shown in the figure on the right, consisted of a lamp contained within a bucket-shaped case with an opaque bottom and cover, and transparent glass sides. It was placed in a line with the keel of the vessel, and could be conveniently hung on the forestay or the top of the mast. When the vessel carrying it was seen end on by another ship, the difference in diameter between the dark bottom and cover of the indicator produced a perfect luminous circle, as shown in the figure below; and when the vessel was seen to port or starboard, the two discs formed crescents of light as shown, the horns of the crescent always pointing in the direction the ship was moving. The final shape was a luminous crosscut in the cover of the indicator, and was only seen when the ship was going astern.

Titanic's Big Sister ... and how she nearly sank

In 1911, the papers were full of exciting news: two new luxury cruise liners were almost ready to embark. The first – and grandest – of these was RMS *Olympic*, the largest ocean liner in the world, which was due to set sail on her maiden voyage to New York on 14 June under the command of the ill-fated Captain Edward Smith. She was owned by the White Star Line, who were also busy building another liner, RMS *Titanic*, which wouldn't be ready to sail until 10 April the following year.

Once unveiled, the *Olympic* became the pride of the British Transatlantic Service. This floating palace was the epitome of luxury, possessing Turkish baths, opulent suites with private bathrooms, elevators, grand saloons, gymnasiums, squash courts, nurseries, swimming pools, roof gardens and even a fishpond. She could carry almost 2,500 passengers and nearly 1,000 crew members. Her grandeur was renowned across the world, and she'd frequently accommodate scores of American millionaires at any one time.

Her fortune, however, looked set to change on 20 September 1911, when a terrible accident occurred: the *Olympic* collided with another ship, *Hawke*, just hours after leaving Southampton. The latter was attempting to overtake the former on the starboard side, but the *Hawke* suddenly veered to port and crashed into the side of the liner, slicing through the metal like a knife through butter. The *Olympic* was seriously damaged and began taking on water, putting the lives of everyone on board in peril. A gaping hole, between 20ft and 40ft long, had been torn into her side, just where the third-class cabins were situated. Had the occupants not been on deck at the time, there would have undoubtedly been dozens of fatalities, but miraculously, not a single person was seriously hurt.

There was great concern at Southampton when the shipping authorities heard of the accident, for there were 732 first class passengers on board *Olympic* – a record number for a ship crossing the Atlantic. Among the VIP passengers were several well-known and highly influential American millionaires. The authorities knew they had to act quickly, and assistance was sent without delay.

The disaster had happened not far from Cowes, on the Isle of Wight, where crowds of people had gathered to watch the spectacle of the *Olympic*'s passing. They all witnessed the crash, which occurred about a mile and a half from land, so it was quite easy for the rescue boats to tug the great liner slowly and painfully back to port.

The majority of passengers, it seemed, were filled with excitement rather than alarm, and were fascinated to get a glimpse of the damage once they'd gone ashore. Apart from the gaping hole, the only other misfortune was that one passenger's suitcase was washed out of the side of the ship, and never recovered. Several other passengers had to make do with soggy luggage, including three English brides-to-be, who were travelling to America to marry their stateside grooms, patiently waiting for them on the other side of the Atlantic. Their dresses had become stained with saltwater, and two of the young women were seriously grieved, but the third was reported to have shrugged off the incident with the words: 'He's waited for me for five years; I think he'll wait a little longer.' There were also a number of complaints lodged by a handful of passengers who were in a hurry to reach New York, but aside from that, the incident passed without lasting notice, and soon slipped out of living memory.

It later transpired that one of the luckiest people travelling on board the *Olympic* that day was a stewardess named Violet Jessop. Following the accident she was transferred from the *Olympic* and sent to work aboard the *Titanic*, surviving the terrible fate that befell the liner on 15 April. She then went to work on board HMHS *Britannic*, the youngest of the three sister ships. Miraculously, she survived when this ship was sunk in the Aegean Sea during the First World War, having struck an underwater mine.

After a long and illustrious career, RMS *Olympic* was sold in 1934 prior to being demolished.

♪ Ships at Sea ♪

Printed in the *Leicester Chronicle*, 21 November 1857

I have ships that went to sea
More than fifty years ago;
None have yet come home to me,
But keep sailing to and fro.
I have seen them in my sleep,
Plunging through the shoreless deep,
With tattered sails and battered hulls,
While around them scream'd the gulls,
Flying low, flying low.

I have wondered why they staid
From me, sailing round the world;
And I have said, 'I'm half afraid
That their sails will ne'er be furl'd.'
Great the treasures that they hold,
Silks, and plumes, and bars of gold,
While the spices which they bear
Fill with fragrance all the air,
As they sail, as they sail.

Every sailor in the port
Knows that I have ships at sea;
Of the waves and winds the sport,
And the sailors pity me.
Oft they come and with me walk,
Cheering me with hopeful talk,
'Till I put my fears aside,
And contented watch the tide
Rise and fall, rise and fall.

I have waited on the piers,
Gazing for them down the bay,
Days and nights for many years,
'Till I turned heart sick away,

But the pilots, when they land,
Stop and take me by the hand,
Saying, 'You will live to see
Your proud vessels come from sea,
One and all, one and all.'

So I never quite despair,
Nor let hope nor courage fail;
And some day, when skies are fair,
Up the bay my ships will sail.
I can buy them all I need,
Prints to look at, books to read,
Horses, wines, and works of art,
Everything, except a heart,
That is lost, that is lost.

Once when I was pure and young,
Poorer, too, than I am now,
Ere a cloud was o'er me flung,
Or a wrinkle crossed my brow,
There was one whose heart was mine,
But she's something now divine,
And, though come my ships from sea,
They can bring no heart to me,
Evermore, evermore.

A Daring Sea Rescue

It was a miserable-looking crew of the British brig *Elite* that landed at the Port of New York on the last day of November in 1897. They were brought ashore by the SS *Exeter City*, having been rescued from their waterlogged craft 250 miles east of St John's, Newfoundland.

According to their American rescuers, the crewmen's tragic tales of a woeful voyage were substantiated by the cuts, bruises, swellings and bandages that covered their emaciated bodies. They told how their vessel, buffeted by stormy seas, sprung a leak, and how the hungry and exhausted men had worked tirelessly at the pumps for days on end to save themselves from watery graves. One of their number perished, and his body was committed to the waves.

In mid-November, the *Elite's* plight had been brought to the attention of the authorities at Baltimore by the SS *Rossmore*, which had been in touch with the doomed vessel and had provided the starving crew with provisions. She was leaking quite badly then, but the proud captain, Mark Robert Hargrave, refused to abandon his vessel, and insisted that the *Rossmore* went on her way.

Then, on 25 November, like a scene from the legend of the *Mary Celeste*, the *Elite* was discovered abandoned and in a state of ruin by the captain of the SS *Veendam*. He ordered his crew to set her alight, as she was a dangerous obstruction to navigation.

The fate of the crew wasn't known until the *Exeter City* arrived at the Port of New York, having rescued the crew from their ill-starred vessel on 24 November. Though the seas were high and stormy, it only took ten minutes for the steamship's lifeboat to rescue the crew. Some of the sailors were so weak that they had to be lifted into the boat.

The *Elite* hailed from the Yorkshire town of Goole, on the river Humber, and was engaged in transporting supplies of fish from the Spanish city of *Cádiz to St John's*. Everything was plain sailing during the first week of the voyage; the only piece of drama occurred on the second day, when the captain discovered a stowaway on board. He was Able Seaman John Thomas Coles, a deserter from a ship at *Cádiz*, who explained that he wanted to reach his sweetheart in St John's, where he was due to be married. Captain Hargrave took pity on the man, and put him straight to work.

Before the end of the second week, it soon became clear that things were not quite as the sailors had expected. For a start, it was discovered that the captain had failed to bring enough provisions aboard, and the discerning ship's cook calculated that they would run out of food and water long before they reached Newfoundland. The men were duly put on short allowance.

Fair weather soon gave way to mighty storms. Crashing waves began to wash over the craft, and the men were unable to keep control of the vessel. She soon began taking on water, at which time all hands were directed to the pumps. As the storms grew wilder, the strength of the starving crew began to fail. Without food and with little sleep, the work became too much. The stowaway, Coles, and a Spanish sailor by the name of Juan Erraseeras, both fell gravely ill.

When the ship was about 300 miles from the coast of St John's, the crew managed to flag down the passing *Rossmore*, which had set sail from Liverpool.

'We are starving!' was the message written on the sails in order to attract help.

A barrel from the *Rossmore*, filled with raw meat and other provisions, was sent out to the *Elite* through the angry sea. The grateful crew began devouring the meat without even the will to cook it, but Captain Hargrave refused further help from the ship, labouring under the belief that he could still make it to his intended port.

Three days later, the storms became decidedly worse. Needing every man at the pumps, the desperate captain ordered the two sick men out of their bunks, but they were too weak to be of any use, so the captain reputedly struck them with a hatchet. Coles fell to the ground, but a fellow shipmate lifted him to his feet and held him to the pump. The Spaniard, on the other hand, fell once and never rose again.

As soon as the five surviving crew members reached New York, they visited the offices of the British Consul and arranged for transportation home. The incident, however, did nothing to discourage Captain Hargrave, and he returned to a life at sea.

The Salcombe Lifeboat Disaster

Arnold Jabez Hargrave was a merchant sea captain from Yorkshire. Born in 1858, he first went to sea at the age of five as his father's cabin boy; and as he grew older he rose through the ranks, eventually becoming master of a fleet of schooners. He travelled the world, transporting salt and other provisions to Europe and beyond, returning via Whitby whenever he could so he could buy a piece of jewellery made of jet for his beloved wife, Caroline.

Captain Hargrave's favourite schooner was called the *Western Lass*. He loved her so much that he commissioned an Italian artist to paint two portraits of her, one in calm waters and the other in a storm. The day he had to give her up, as his retirement approached, was one of the saddest of his life. It seemed that the *Western Lass* may have harboured similar feelings for her master, for she ran aground shortly after her new captain took command.

It was late in the night on Thursday, 26 October 1916. The schooner and her crew of six were voyaging from Swansea to the French port of Caen, carrying a cargo of coal, when they ran into difficulty and became wrecked on Meg Rock, close to Prawle Point, Devon. They sent out a distress signal, and within a few hours the Prawle Rocket Company dispatched a team of rescuers who fired a safety line towards the ship, which the sailors were able to scramble along. All the crew reached the shore safely, alive but badly shaken.

In the meantime, an alarm was raised at Salcombe Harbour when the wreckage of the *Western Lass* was spotted. Assuming the crew were still in peril, a lifeboat named *William and Emma* was sent out around dawn. Though a furious gale was raging, this didn't worry the fifteen experienced sailors on board. The majority of them were married with families, but they put aside any concerns for their own safety and bravely battled the clashing tides.

Upon reaching the crewless schooner, it became clear their services weren't required. They set off back towards Salcombe, but they never made it: a tremendous breaker capsized the lifeboat at about 10.40 am, and all fifteen men were cast into the sea. Some of them managed to cling on to the underside of their boat, but the waves lashed them off again and again. Another lifeboat was sent out and two men were saved, but all the others were lost. Only three bodies were recovered for burial; the sea claimed the other ten.

♪ A Prayer by the Sea ♪

Sarah Doudney

Printed in *The Hull Packet and East Riding Times*, 15 August 1884

I saw the ship on a windy sea,
In the light of the morning's gold;
And the shout of the sailors came to me
Like songs from the days of old.

Wild waves leapt up on the crag and beat
On the edge of the rock-bound shore,
And the thought of a coming time was sweet
When the sea should be no more.

No more, no more, shall mothers and wives
Dream of loves that the blue wastes hide,
No more shall the vigorous hearts and lives
Be flung to the wind and tide!

Oh, Father, follow the gallant ships
Through the light of the morning pale!
Thou hearest the pray of the loving lips;
Thy mercy can never fail.

And guide us all to some haven blest
Where never a tempest is known,
For life is sad, and the secret of rest
Is hidden with Thee alone.

The Loss of the *White Ship* and why Henry I Never Smiled Again

Over the course of history, countless disasters have befallen ships attempting to cross the busy English Channel. In 1896, 247 lives were lost when the cruise liner SS *Drummond Castle* was wrecked as a result of the captain's careless navigation. Just three years later, the mail boat *Stella* was sunk; and in 1878, HMS *Eurydice* went down in a storm off the coast of the Isle of Wight, killing more than 300 men on board.

It could be argued, though, that none of these incidents come close to surpassing a tragedy that occurred in the English Channel long before the Age of Steam. It concerned the well-known *White Ship*, a state-of-the-art medieval galley that was considered nothing less than a triumph of naval architecture. She was built by Thomas FitzStephen, son of Stephen FitzAirard, who captained William the Conqueror's flagship, *Mora*, during his 1066 invasion of England; and the loss of the *White Ship* came to be remembered as one of the worst naval catastrophes in peacetime history.

It was 25 November 1120, and King Henry I, who'd been visiting Normandy with his family and courtiers, was due to return home to England. FitzStephen offered the king the use of the *White Ship*, but the monarch had already made travel arrangements. He was impressed by the vessel, however, and accepted it on behalf of his beloved son and heir apparent, Prince William. It was thus arranged that William, accompanied by several hundred attendees, would follow his father across the Channel on board the *White Ship*, but not before the young prince had taken full advantage of all the luxuries this medieval party boat could offer.

Stepping on deck that autumnal afternoon, as the ship swayed in the harbour of Barfleur, the Crown Prince cheerily waved his father's galley away, and as she faded into the distance, a signal was given for the merriment to commence. Determined to make the most of the king's absence, William and his courtiers cast away propriety and allowed gaiety to reign. Their antics became progressively wilder as the alcohol stores grew dry. Round and round went the flagons of wine, and everyone on board, from the prince to the oarsmen, became rolling drunk. Captain FitzStephen was so intoxicated he could barely see in a straight line, let alone navigate a smooth course across the tempestuous English Channel.

It was customary at that time for a priest to bless a vessel prior to departure, but the revellers were having none of this, and refused to allow piety to spoil the party. When the zealous minister arrived, he was sent away with a flea in his ear.

As the sun began its descent and the shadows of night started to creep over the rooftops of Normandy, the officers in charge of guarding the prince's treasure became concerned and insisted that the captain made haste. The unblessed galley set off into the darkness, and the noble merrymakers were eager to make up for lost time. Though the king was hours ahead of them, the partygoers urged FitzStephen to attempt to overtake him. The *White Ship* was the fastest vessel of her kind; and with their confidence boosted by copious amounts of alcohol, the captain and crew were certain they'd be able to reach the shores of England first. Fifty well-oiled oarsmen duly took their places and steered the ship straight into a submerged rock, one that sober mariners usually remembered to avoid.

High spirits turned to horror as carnage broke loose. The ship capsized so quickly that there was only time to launch a single boat. The prince was hastily bundled into it, and it seemed for a time that he was going to escape with his life, but he heard the cries of his half-sister, Matilda FitzRoy, Countess of Perche (an illegitimate daughter of King Henry I), and turned his boat around. In his attempt to reach the foundering wreckage, he was swamped by dozens of people trying to save themselves, and the heir to the throne of England was drowned.

Only three people out of 300 resurfaced alive that night; one was FitzStephen. He managed to cling on tightly to the mast, and might just have made it to safety had he not learned that the prince had perished. Preferring to face death than the king's wrath, he let go of the mast and was lost beneath the waves.

When the king was informed of his son's death he was plunged into a deep state of mourning from which he never recovered. The whole of England, too, descended into civil turmoil as the two main claimants to the throne – the king's legitimate daughter, Empress Matilda, and her cousin, Stephen of Blois – fought for their right to rule. After Henry's death in 1135 it was Stephen who took the throne, but it was Matilda's son, Henry II, who eventually inherited the crown.

Hermetically Sealed Inside a Shipwreck

On 18 April 1903, Captain Hans Engellandt, of the German cargo ship *Erndte*, set sail from Memel, in modern-day Lithuania. His voyage to Oldenburg, Germany, took him across the Baltic Sea, where a violent gale was raging. Though the wind was howling and sleet was lashing down upon him, Captain Engellandt remained at the helm until about four o'clock the following morning, when he went below deck to change his saturated clothes.

Just as he'd donned some fresh underwear the ship suddenly capsized, and the captain found himself standing on the roof of his cabin. Though the sea had flooded the vessel and the rest of the crew had perished, the captain's cabin had become hermetically sealed, providing him with enough air to survive and the ship with enough buoyancy to stay afloat.

By loosening the ceiling boards, which had now become the floor, the captain was able to gain access to a store room, and he managed to salvage a few tins of condensed milk, 3lb of prunes, a quantity of rice sugar, some sausages and a hammer. For twelve days he survived in his sealed cabin, eating the food sparingly and hammering on the steel bottom of the ship to attract the attention of any vessels that happened to be passing.

On 1 May he heard a welcome noise: footsteps walking above him! At long last someone had happened upon the wreck. He leapt to his feet and again began hammering on the ceiling – which had once been the floor – and to his relief his rescuers began boring a hole into the ship. He was able to peer through, and learned that his saviours had come from a Norwegian steamer, the *Aurora*. They'd spotted the *Erndte* and had been attempting to tow the wreck away when they heard the captive's knocks.

Captain Engellandt informed them he'd enough food left to last him for another four days, and duly instructed them to plug the hole, for he feared his ship would sink completely if too much air escaped from his cabin. He then asked the crewmen to tow his ship back to land, for he could see no way of being released while the *Erndte* was still in the open sea. The Norwegian sailors were happy to oblige, and the wreck safely arrived at the Polish port of Neufahrwasser, where the captain was cut free.

♪ A Song of the Sea ♪

William Cox Bennett
Published in *Songs for Sailors*, 1872

'Sailor, sailor, tell to me
What sights have you seen on the mighty sea?'

'When the seas were calm and the skies were clear,
And the watch I've kept until day was near,
Eyes I have seen, black as yours, dear, are,
And a face I've looked on that was, how far!
That was, girl, oh! how far from me!'

'Sailor, sailor, tell to me
What else have you seen on the far, far sea?'

'I've seen the flying-fish skim the brine,
And the great whales below, and these eyes of mine
Have seen on the icebergs the north-lights play –
But often I've seen a home far away,
And a girl, oh, how dear to me!'

'Sailor, sailor, tell to me
The sounds men hear on the stormy sea.'

'I've heard, my girl, the wild winds blow,
And the good ship creak to her keel below;
But a laugh, too, I've heard, that, O well, well I know!
And a far, far voice – a voice that was, O
How sweet! O how sweet to me!'

'Nay tell me, sailor, tell to me
The sights and scenes of the wild, wild sea.'

'Alike in calm, and breeze, and storm
I've dream'd one dream, and I've seen one form;
One dream that, dearest, shall soon be true,
One form that, my girl, I clasp in you,
That my own sweet wife shall be.'

How to Raise Sunken Ships

Over the centuries, tales of sunken treasure ships have captured the public's imagination. Newspapers and magazines regularly featured stories and legends about gold-laden wrecks that supposedly littered the sandy beds of the seven seas. On 21 October 1869, for example, Liverpool's *Daily Post* reported that the passenger ship *Hamilla Mitchell*, which was wrecked in the China Sea on 10 August that year, was carrying a cargo of goods estimated to have been worth £140,000, a value the equivalent of approximately £11,550,000 today. As tempting as this sounded to treasure hunters, submarine technology was still in its infancy, so reaching these floundered vessels – and the supposed fortunes therein – proved challenging.

This was set to change in 1880, when it was announced that an Australian engineer had devised an ingenious way of raising sunken ships from the depths of the ocean. His method involved securing a bottle of sulphuric acid inside a deflated balloon, along with a highly reactive chemical known as Bullrich's salt. The contraption was then sent down into the ocean and attached to an easily accessible part of the sunken ship. By turning a stopcock, the bottle was mechanically opened, releasing the acid into the balloon. As the liquid mingled with the salt, a chemical reaction occurred, causing carbon dioxide to fill and inflate the balloon. It thereby followed that if enough balloons were secured to the vessel, it would gradually rise to the surface, allowing scientists, explorers and treasure seekers alike the opportunity to thoroughly and conveniently examine the wreckage on dry land.

Trials were conducted on the Plötzensee Lake in Berlin, where a small sunken craft was successfully raised to the surface; and it was hoped that this method of raising sunken ships would be of great service to the nautical world in the not-too-distant future.

The Voyage that Lasted a Century

In 1932, a mysterious ship was sighted at Steenberg Cove, St Helena Bay, off the coast of South Africa, the place she was destined to make port 100 years earlier. She never finished her voyage, for she was looted and burned by pirates before being wrecked at the bottom of the ocean. Despite this, she somehow managed to rise to the surface of the waves once more, in a seemingly desperate bid to complete her passage.

Custom officials made careful examinations of the barnacle-encrusted vessel, but nothing of note was found. There was no cargo aboard, and the wreck was eventually brought ashore, as it constituted a danger to shipping.

♪ The Sailor's Farewell ♪

Julia Goddard
Printed in *The Derby Mercury*, 26 January 1876

The anchor's weighed, the sails unfurled,
Our flag is floating free;
And away we sail with the summer gale
Far over the golden sea;
Far, far away, to another world,
That lies in the glittering West;
And I'll bring my darling the treasure home
That I know will please her best.
Yoho! heave ho, my boys, heave ho!
The wind is fair, and away we go.

Blue eyes are weeping upon the shore
For the sailor on the main,
And there's never a day but a soul will pray
That he may come home again;
And whether the wind blows loud or low
O'er the raging of the sea,
That prayer will float, like a silver note,
And bring a blessing to me.
Yoho! heave ho! 'tis hard to part,
But we shall meet again, sweetheart.

What is the treasure, O maiden mine –
Is it coral, or pearl, or gold,
Or silken band, or shells from the strand
That foreign waves enfold?
All these I'll bring for my maiden fair –
But ah! she will like the best
A heart that ne'er had a thought but of her
Since I sailed for the golden West.
Yoho! heave ho! 'tis hard to part,
But we shall meet again, sweetheart.

Desert Island Risks

Film lovers may recall the 2000 movie *Cast Away*, in which Tom Hanks's character becomes stranded on a desert island for four years. Though the alarming plotline may seem implausible, such a scenario did actually happened to three Englishmen more than 100 years ago.

'FOUR YEARS ON A DESERT ISLAND', declared a headline in *The Western Times*. The article, published on 27 February 1890, explained how the three unfortunate passengers, along with a handful of crew members, set sail in October 1885 on board a small Japanese vessel, *Matsum Marie*, but as they crossed the Straits of Tsugaru, between the Sea of Japan and the Pacific Ocean, the ship was blown hundreds of miles off course by a cyclone.

The men were lost at sea for eighty days, drifting aimlessly through the ocean until they finally reached the uninhabited island of San Alesandro, which later became known as Kita Iwo Jima, or North Sulphur Island. Five crew members drowned as they attempted to swim to shore, and the remaining sailors, not wanting to die on a volcanic island, attempted to repair their damaged lifeboat once they'd landed. Though the craft was leaking badly and provisions were scarce, they set sail again in search of rescue. The three Englishmen, however, refused to re-enter the craft, so they were left alone on the island, hoping that salvation would come swiftly, but they were profoundly disappointed.

For four long years the men survived on fruit and sea birds. They fashioned fishing hooks from the metal workings of their watches, and spent their days gazing on, helplessly, as sailing ships passed them by on the distant horizon, too far away to spot any signals for help. The castaways endured terrible injuries and adversities; and when a passing American vessel picked them up, in February 1890, the men 'presented quite a wild appearance'. Their hair hung down below their shoulders, and their clothes had been reduced to rags. They'd been able to flag down the ship by fastening a white shirt to the top of the tallest tree, which they'd stripped of its branches. The shirt blew in the wind for several hours before it was spotted by the American crew.

This wasn't the only documented case of shipwrecked castaways learning how to survive on uninhabited desert islands. On 18 January 1894, *The Southern Reporter* described how a handful of survivors were washed ashore on the inhospitable Antipodes Island, about 530 miles south of New Zealand, following the loss of their trading ship, *Spirit of the Dawn*, on 4 September the previous year. The English crew had been transporting a cargo of rice from Rangoon, Burma, to Talcahuano, Chile, when the vessel struck some rocks during a thick fog. The ship began to sink at an alarming rate, so the crew began to climb the rigging. Several men, including the captain, were drowned, and some officers managed to escape in the only lifeboat they'd taken with them. A passing ship rescued eleven of the floundering sailors, who'd spent several hours in the water; the few surviving men who remained in the sea were washed up on the rocky volcanic island when morning came.

For eighty days these castaways lived on 'raw mutton, birds, penguins' eggs, and roots, without any fire'. Like the survivors on San Alesandro, they spotted several ships passing the island, though they were too far away to flag down.

The winter nights began drawing in, and as bitter winds blew in from Antarctica the weather took a turn for the worse. Just when the survivors' cause began to look hopeless, a steamer from New Zealand spotted the men and picked them up, but not before one of the stranded sailors lost a toe through frostbite.

Perhaps one of the most alarming castaway stories of all was brought to the public's attention in 1888, when an elderly gentleman from Brooklyn received a curious letter on 11 September, seemingly from beyond the grave. The correspondent was a good friend of his named Captain Green, who'd been presumed dead, having gone down with his ship in 1858. The letter confirmed that this wasn't the case; in fact, the captain was very much alive, having been living on an uninhabited island for the past thirty years! His ship, the *Confederation*, had set sail from New York, bound for Australia, but the crew never reached their destination, and nothing more was heard from them.

The letter, dated July 1887, had been written on a soiled page from a ship's logbook, and had somehow found its way on to a whaling barque. Its captain duly delivered the letter to its intended recipient, who made no hesitation in communicating its contents to the national press.

Captain Green explained to his friend that his ship sank during a terrible gale. There were sixteen crew members and two female passengers on board, and all of them managed to escape in lifeboats. After forty days they landed on a coral-reefed island in the South Seas, which the captain explained was named Ojee. Though there were no signs of human habitation, the mystery island abounded with game, fish, fruit and fresh running water, which kept them sustained until 1862.

It was in this year when the captain and his fellow castaways spotted a vessel, the first one they'd seen since they were stranded. Though it was nothing more than a speck on the horizon, some of the company decided to return to the lifeboat in which they'd landed and set out towards the ship; but the sea was high, and the eight brave men were drowned.

The remaining ten survivors began to accept their fate, and settled down to a life on a desert island. Two of the sailors married the female passengers, and children were born. Though there were a few deaths within the community, by 1887 the settlers numbered twelve in all, and the captain expected their number to grow. He explained in his letter that everyone was quite content with their new situation, and although it would have been nice to have some new clothes, life was satisfactory.

The captain ended his letter by noting he was 68 years old, and still in good health.

A similar tale was published in the *Evening Telegraph & Star and Sheffield Daily Times* on 27 November 1888. Led by Professor Lee, a naturalist of Bowdoin College, Maine, the crew of the *Albatross* arrived at Charles Island of the Galápagos. Expecting it to be uninhabited, save for a few wild animals that were ripe for scientific study, the crew were astonished to stumble across an extremely aged, gaunt and semi-naked man. His grey beard was long and unkempt, and he'd lived on the island for so long that he'd grown 'almost as

wild as the animals among whom he lived'. It wasn't clear to the explorers just how long he'd been resident there, but they deduced it must have been decades since he'd last laid eyes on another human face, for the man was fearful, rather than joyful, when he saw them.

It took several hours for the hermit to learn to trust his new visitors, but eventually he was able to communicate parts of his story to them. He explained that it was long ago when his ship came ashore. He and a party of researchers had gone to the island to search for a prized species of moss, but the group had become separated, and his companions eventually left the island without him. Determined to survive, he set about making a comfortable life for himself, surviving on fruit and herbs, and building a shelter from wood and animal skins. Though he'd grown accustomed to his solitary way of life, it didn't take the scientists long to persuade the man to return with them to civilization.

The Castaway Community

It was 9 May 1820 when the fishing vessel *Princess of Wales* sailed from London towards the small, volcanic Prince Edward Island, a place situated about 1,370 miles south of South Africa, where sea life was plentiful. The ship and her crew finally made it to the Indian Ocean on 17 March the following year, but they went no further: at midnight the vessel was wrecked against the rocks of the Crozet Islands, some way from the intended destination. The captain felt it would be better to go down with the *Princess* rather than risk starvation and other agonies on some forsaken islet, but the crew eventually persuaded him to get into the lifeboat, and together they made land long before daybreak.

With nowhere else to hide from the carnivorous elephant seals that lived in huge numbers on the island, the seven castaways spent the remaining hours of the night huddling underneath their boat.

The morning sun cast light over the scene of the disaster. Fortunately for the survivors, the wreckage of the *Princess of Wales* was within relatively easy reach, and they spent the day salvaging what they could from the debris. They managed to retrieve a few chests of soggy bread, some sails, a bit of rigging and the ship's mast, as well as a tinderbox, a frying pan, a gridiron, a lance, a Bible and a few pieces of cutlery.

Though the company tried to erect a shelter with their salvaged material, the stormy weather made their task impossible, and so they were forced to spend the next three weeks living underneath their lifeboat. They filled their days with Bible reading and hunting seabirds and elephant seals. By the fourth week they'd succeeded in building a hut, covering the roof with animal skins and the floor with moss, and using soft grass for their bedding. The clothes they were wearing lasted until December, when they were compelled to make themselves new garments out of sealskins, sewed together with threads made from animal sinews.

Before the year 1822 had dawned, the company were overjoyed to see a small boat sailing around the shore. The vessel, containing eight sailors, landed on the beach, and the castaways were astonished to learn that their new visitors had also been shipwrecked a few months ago on a neighbouring island. They'd found their home less than satisfactory, however, and had set sail in search of a more comfortable abode.

The fifteen companions settled down in harmony together, and resolved to pool their resources to build a more permanent settlement. They succeeded in erecting huts made of stone, and during their forages came across some ruined wooden shelters that had become buried in the sand. It was presumed that they'd been built by American sailors who'd once visited the island. The settlers decided to put the wood to good use, and within five months they'd built themselves a 12-ton ship. The future suddenly looked rosy, but on the evening of the vessel's launch she was blown against the rocks and destroyed.

Scarcely had this misfortune occurred when one of the castaways called out: 'A sail!'

All heads turned to the horizon, but nothing more than the white flash of a gull's wing was observed. The castaway, however, was certain he'd seen a ship, so the men lit an enormous bonfire, the light from which must have been visible for miles around. Sure enough, a schooner appeared, and it sent out a small boat to investigate the source of the flames.

The shipwrecked seamen couldn't believe their eyes, and as one they began running towards the approaching vessel. Their ill-fitting sealskin trousers parted company with their legs before they'd made it to the edge of the beach.

The crew of the schooner, upon being greeted in such a feral manner, mistook the wild-haired semi-naked gathering for indigenous tribesmen, and were too intimidated to venture any closer.

The castaways barely had the time, or the inclination, to offer an introduction. They were so desperate for rescue that they ran straight into the sea and began swimming towards the schooner, where they were brought on board and provided with every necessity required. They were taken to Mauritius and from there transported back home to England, and reunited with their families at long last.

♪ A First Love-Making ♪

Lucy Clifford
Printed in *Family Magazine*, 1885

A land there is beyond the sea
That I have never seen,
But Johnny says he'll take me there
And I shall be a queen.
He'll build for me a palace there,
Its roof will be of thatch,
And it will have a little porch
And everything to match.

And he'll give me a garden-green,
And he'll give me a crown
Of flowers that love the wood and field
And never grow in town.
And we shall be so happy there,
And never, never part,
And I shall be the grandest queen –
The queen of Johnny's heart.

Then, Johnny, man your little boat
To sail across the sea;
There's only room for king and queen –
For Johnny and for me.
And, Johnny dear, I'm not afraid
Of any wind or tide,
For I am always safe, my dear,
If you are by my side.

The Twice Unlucky Mariner

In about 1795, a British ship named *Daedalus* sailed from Port Jackson, Australia, to Otaheite (later Tahiti), a small island in the South Seas, where, for the past three decades, good trading links had been established between the indigenous people and the West. When the crew of the *Daedalus* landed, they were surprised to find nine Englishmen living with the Tahitians. They'd married and had settled down on the island with their new families.

Despite their seemingly comfortable situation, the Englishmen were actually castaways who'd been shipwrecked on the island some time earlier. They were rescued and taken in by the natives, who knew a little of the English language, having become accustomed to white traders visiting their shores. The sailors were treated like dignitaries, and having been nursed back to health the Tahitians bestowed upon them land, servants and even wives. As a sign of their elevated position, the castaways were tattooed from head to toe with native symbols denoting their inferred superiority.

Though eight of the Englishmen were quite happy with this cushy new life, there was one sailor who yearned for home. In fact, when the *Daedalus* turned up he was first on board, and couldn't wait to return to England.

Sadly for him, he was destined to never set foot on English soil again, for as soon as the ship pulled into port on the Thames, a press gang seized him and carried him away to a warship, where he was forced to spend the rest of his working days.

The Press-Ganged Groom

During the prosperous Age of Sail, which lasted from the sixteenth to the nineteenth century, the British Navy was one of the largest, most successful navies in the world. Determined to remain so, the navy employed so-called press gangs to swell their crews during times of war. These fearsome gangs of men would travel round towns and cities, and would generally use nefarious means to force fit, eligible men, usually ones with seafaring experience, to work on board warships. So prolific was the practice that 217 of the sailors who fought on HMS *Victory* at the Battle of Trafalgar in 1805 were press-ganged; they accounted for about 26 per cent of the entire crew.

In early 1729, Britain was growing fearful that Spain had serious designs on Jamaica, a British colony. Reports had reached England that teams of

Spaniards had been committing terrible depredations in the West Indies, so the Royal Navy sent a man-of-war to the island in order to deter the aggressors. It worked, but the authorities knew that more men would be needed in the event of further action, so the press gangs got to work.

In Newcastle on Saturday, 16 April, they accosted a young man on the steps of a church, where he was about to marry his sweetheart. Just as they were dragging him away to their ship, the bride-to-be pleaded with the gang to at least allow her beau a few moments to get married. They refused, explaining that they were a religious press gang, and believed it was a sin to part a man and wife.

♪ The Pirate ♪

John B. Pedler

Printed in *The North Wales Chronicle*, 8 July 1853

The Pirate is – (what shall I say?)
A robber on the sea:
He pilfers craft, by craft, to-day,
To-morrow, he is free –
He scruples not, to plan and plot,
Tho' murder stains his soul;
A ship he spies, he onward hies
To reach the destin'd goal.

Arm'd to the teeth, on deck he stands
A tyrant on the waves;
Aye, there he stands, with blood stain'd hands,
And death and danger braves –
On, on he sails, the ship he hails
Surrender or you die;
Strike! strike he cries, for once be wise,
'Tis useless now to fly.

The merchantman still skims along,
In hopes to 'scape the foe;
Meanwhile her crew, like Britons true
Are arm'd to strike the blow –
The Privateer still draws more near
The craft she deems her prize;
On, on she steers, while deaf'ning cheers
Re-echo to the skies.

Once more, the pirate Captain hails
The flying craft to yield;
She, heeds it not, on, on she flies
O'er ocean's hedgeless field –
On, on she flies, while British eyes
Look on from heads reclined;
To gaze on those, relentless foes –
Scarce pistol shot behind.

A flash is seen, a sound is heard,
A something whistles by;
The British Captain gives the word
We'll conquer or we'll die.
Take steady aim to kill and maim
As many as you can;
Fire, fire away, we'll win the day,
We'll leave them not a man.

The silence which had reign'd before
On board the destin'd prize,
Had chang'd the peaceful garb it wore
To greet her enemies –
With arming brief the pirate chief
Who ne'er was beat before;
Was sent to sleep, 'neath the briny deep,
To sleep, to 'wake no more.

The pirate crew, they still fought on,
Their godless ends to gain;
But God who dearly loves his own
Had doom'd their efforts vain –
The Privateer, tho' once so near,
Now slowly lagg'd behind;–
While British tars, unseath'd by scars,
Were borne before the wind.

The sequel now, its tale must tell,
In language, strong and true:
The privateer, her end is near,
She's sinking from the view –
She's sinking fast, too fast to last,
She soon must settle down:
And a briny grave, 'neath the ocean wave
Her robber crew must own.

The bosom, scarce to thought gave birth,
When lo! a shriek was heard;
One bitter wail, and every sail,
For ever disappear'd
The British Captain breath'd a sigh,
His bosom felt a pain,
When the pirate crew all sank from view
'Neath the breast of the restless main.

The Discovery of Smugglers' Caves

In 1886, a man named Reverend H.A. Thorne was stunned to discover an extensive subterranean labyrinth beneath his garden in the Kent village of Birchington-on-Sea. The reverend was drawing water from his well when his bucket, which was swaying from side to side, suddenly disappeared from view. Upon inspection, he discovered a hole in the side of his well, large enough for him to climb into. There he discovered a maze of caverns, estimated to measure 20,000 cubic feet in space. It transpired that these caverns had once been constructed and used by smugglers to conceal their contraband goods, which came in from the sea.

A decade later, a similar cave was discovered near Dover. A farmer was busy ploughing his field when the ground suddenly subsided, almost causing his horse to fall into the subterranean cavern that had suddenly been exposed to the light of day. Investigations revealed that at the beginning of the century a smuggler used to live on the site where the farmhouse stood. Before the area was cleared for farmland it was covered by a thick, dark forest, making it an ideal place for smugglers to carry out their clandestine trade. The cavern that the farmer discovered was used as a storehouse by the resident smuggler for his prohibited imports.

Later, in 1924, it was reported in various publications that another smugglers' cave was unearthed, this one at a place called Water Comb Farm just outside Seaton, Devonshire. The farmer's son, Mr Frank Salter, was working the land when his horse's leg became trapped in a fissure in the ground. Upon freeing the beast an expansive cave was discovered beneath the field, in which a collection of coins, dated 1790, were found.

She-Pirates of the Spanish Main

During the early part of the eighteenth century, the Spanish Main was infested with pirates. It later transpired that at least two of their number were females in disguise, though no one suspected a thing, for they were just as lawless and fearsome as their male counterparts.

One of these women was called Mary Read, who was born in England in the 1690s, the younger of two children. Mary's mother was a sailor's widow, who fell pregnant with her first child, a son, shortly before Mr Read set sail on a voyage from which he never returned. Mrs Read fell into another man's bed soon after her husband was lost at sea, and Mary was the product of this illicit encounter.

To hide the shame, she kept Mary a secret from her wealthy in-laws in London; but when her infant son died, and the young widow found herself in financial difficulties, she dressed Mary in boy's clothes and travelled to the capital city in search of support. She visited her late husband's elderly mother and, pretending that Mary was her grandson, pleaded for assistance. The deception was successful, and Mrs Read received a weekly allowance for the rest of her mother-in-law's life.

Mary was 13 years old when her 'grandmother' died, but by then she'd grown used to – and, indeed, rather fond of – donning male attire during her frequent trips to London. Finding herself in need of a new source of income, Mary pretended to be a footboy and entered the employ of a French lady, but the work was dull and tiresome for a young girl who longed for fortune and adventure, so she found work as a cabin boy on board a man-of-war. A life in the military called, and after serving in a regiment of foot as young cadet, and then later the cavalry, she set sail for a new life in the West Indies, but the ship was seized by pirates. With little chance of a promotion in her current position, Mary decided to abscond, and joined the brutal band of buccaneers. Over the years she earned herself a fearsome reputation, and was said to have slain many a man in her quest for riches and notoriety.

One day, in around 1718, Mary's ship was apprehended by another band of pirates, headed by Captain Jack Rackham, who, as fate would have it, also had an imposter within his crew. Her name was Anne Bonny, and she was rumoured to have been the captain's secret lover.

Like Mary, Anne was illegitimate. She'd been born in Ireland to a wealthy attorney and his housemaid, and the family later immigrated to a plantation in South Carolina, where Anne grew up. As a young woman in the early 1700s, she married a pirate named James Bonny, much to the disapproval of her father. She and her new husband eloped together, and fled to the Island of Providence, where Anne made the acquaintance of Captain Rackham. Tempted by the pirate's way of life, Anne disguised herself as a man and joined his motley crew.

The two women felt an instant connection, and soon became firm friends aboard Captain Rackham's ship. However, their close bond of friendship didn't go unnoticed by the jealous captain, who feared that another man was stealing Anne's affections away from him. After threatening Mary with violence, she was forced to reveal her true identity to him. From that day forth the trio cruised in harmony, sharing the two women's secret between them as they went about their pillaging.

Over the years the pirates captured a great number of ships bound to and from England, relieving them all of their cargoes. On board one of these plundered vessels was a young English gentleman whom the buccaneers took into custody. So polite and handsome was he that Mary couldn't help falling in love with him. One day she was horrified to learn that one of her shipmates, after quarrelling with the attractive prisoner, had challenged him to a duel. The Englishman accepted, and though Mary admired his bravery, she knew he was no match for the pirate, who was as mean and ruthless as they came. Two hours before the appointed time of the duel, she deliberately argued with her shipmate over some trivial incident or other, and after a swift sword and pistol fight left him dead, thus sparing the life of the Englishman.

It was October 1720 when the pirates' buccaneering ways finally caught up with them. After a night of celebrations, following their recent victories at Point Negril in Jamaica, Captain Rackham's ship was attacked by one of His Majesty's naval sloops. Fearing for their lives, the pirates fled to the hold; Anne and Mary were the only two crew members brave enough to remain on deck. They called for assistance, labelling their shipmates 'cowards' and insisting that they came and fought 'like men', but no one answered their call; they were left to face the British alone. After a brave but futile stand, everyone on board was arrested and sentenced to death.

Mary Reid died in prison in 1721 before she had to face the hangman's noose. As for Anne, no record of her execution appears to exist. It's often said that her wealthy father, upon hearing of her fate, paid for her release, and she started a new, law-abiding life on a quiet island in the Caribbean. Other versions of the story hold that she settled down in the south of England and bought the lease of a tavern, where she took great delight in enthralling her punters with tales of her daring adventures at sea.

Whatever her fate, the legend of Anne Bonny and Mary Read lives on to this day.

♪ The Pirate's Song ♪

Printed in *The Bristol Mercury*, 24 June 1843

The ocean is mine, and I take what I can
Of the wealth that I find on the wave;
I spurn the control of dominion of man,
Mine's the life of the free and the brave!
I sail where I like,
And never I strike
My flag to another, d'ye see;
O'er my billowy home
Unfetter'd I roam –
Death or Liberty, boys, for me!

My ship is my throne, and wherever I go
Mankind my authority own;
No mortal I fear – no rival I know,
Triumphant I wander alone;
O'er the turbulent deep
My watch still I keep,
And I pounce like a hawk on my prey;
Every man bends his knee
To the King of the Sea,
And homage and tribute they pay.

O, the life that I lead is as free as the breeze,
Wealth and glee with me ever abound;
My merry men share in the spoils that I seize,
And fame is with us always found.
Then, boys, lend an ear,
To my flag gather near –
'Tis the flag of the bold and the brave;
O, come o'er the sea,
And be happy and free,
And sail with the King of the Wave!

Polite Pirates

Since days of old, parents have raised children on swashbuckling stories of history and adventure, in which ruthless pirates, like Captain Hook and Long John Silver, are feared and reviled. At the turn of the twentieth century such barbarous men had long since been confined to the pages of literature, but the First World War heralded the arrival of a new breed of buccaneer: the polite pirate.

An altogether thrilling wartime story was told in the spring of 1915 by the crew of the steamer *Delmira*. After an exhausting chase, the British ship was finally captured by a German submarine in the English Channel, just off the coast of the Isle of Wight.

Delmira was commanded by Captain Lanceford. She had a crew of thirty-two able seamen, who spotted the submarine early one morning. The

Germans fired three revolver shots as a signal to stop, but Captain Lanceford ignored the warning and ordered full steam ahead. The efforts of the crew were no match for the swift submarine, however, and the German pillagers came alongside. To the astonishment of the British, the Germans were most polite indeed, offering their captives wine and ensuring that all the crewmen were safely stowed in the lifeboats before looting the *Delmira* and blowing her to smithereens. The submarine towed the boats for an hour and a half before they eventually spotted a passing British ship that was able to provide rescue.

Three months later, another German submarine sunk the British trawler *Young Percy*. The ship was boarded by the crew of the submarine, who, like the others, were extremely courteous and cordial. They handed out cigarettes to the British sailors and offered them the opportunity to collect some belongings before they were asked very politely to disembark. The brigands proceeded to raid the ship before blowing her up.

One German submarine commander, Lieutenant Von Weddingen, was so hospitable when raiding Allied ships that the British press christened him 'The Polite Pirate'. Armed with a revolver, he always apologized for robbing his victims, making sure to offer them wine and cigars in return. Before departing he'd be sure to ask the British officers to extend his compliments to Lord Churchill. The British Admiralty repaid the favour by blowing up the lieutenant's submarine in March 1915. The Polite Pirate went down with his craft, along with all of his crew.

In 1916, the British steamship *Dresden* was captured by yet another enemy submarine. The British described the German commander as the model of politeness. He apologized profusely that the necessities of war compelled him to destroy the vessel, and expressed his deepest regret at having to subject the crewmen to the inconvenience of returning to Blighty in their lifeboats. He even relieved his captives of their valuables in a polite manner, apologizing for taking £27 10s from Captain Wright. Before they parted company, he insisted on handing the British officer a receipt for the money, made out in the name of the German government.

Another British ship, the *Bute*, was destroyed in the July of that year. The German commander was just as polite, expressing regret for having to sink the ship, and handing out warm tea and cigarettes to all the crewmen. He further apologized when he realized he had no milk for the tea.

The *Derby Daily Telegraph* reported in 1922 that a band of swarthy seafarers had politely hijacked a Mediterranean ship, taking diamond rings from female passengers and kissing the hands from which they'd removed the valuables. The following year, the British steamer *Hydrangea* was attacked by pirates on her voyage from Hong Kong to the Chinese port of Shantou. There were 500 passengers on board, along with 300 tons of cargo. Two days after Christmas, at seven o'clock in the evening, a band of armed pirates boarded the vessel and took control, navigating her to the notorious pirate hideout known as Bias Bay, off the coast of Hong Kong. Nobody was harmed, and during the unexpected detour the pirates tended to the every comfort of the British officers, who were being held hostage in the saloon. The hijackers offered their captives fruit and cigarettes, and even warm blankets, before making off with £700 worth of cargo. This was seemingly enough for the bandits, and before they left, they were courteous enough to return the cash they'd previously taken from the passengers.

Contrary to popular belief, this was all in accordance with the traditional pirate code of courtesy. Over the centuries, even the most fearsome pirates have been known to raise a glass and drink to their victims' health; some even provided hostages with clean shirts before making them walk the plank. One particular marauder of the seas was said to have commissioned a decorative mahogany plank that was tastefully carved. He insisted it was polished before every use, as he didn't want his victims to judge him too unfavourably.

The Lost Treasure of Alborán

In 1906, a daring company of treasure seekers set sail from Plymouth aboard the small yacht *Alkelda*, bound for the Spanish island of Alborán. They'd heard and believed the testimony of an aged sailor named Robinson, who, as a young lad, used to sail the seven seas aboard a vessel named the *Young Constitution* with a band of ruthless pirates.

It was 1831 when, according to Robinson, the buccaneers made a hasty retreat from Jamaica, for the British Navy were hot on their tail. Desperate to avoid capture, the pirates sailed from the West Indies towards the Mediterranean, and happening upon a small uninhabited island, they landed and buried a vast quantity of gold and jewels to the value of £1,000,000. They resumed their voyage but were captured shortly afterwards. Each and every one was hanged, save for the young lad Robinson, who managed to evade the noose. He lived with his dark secret for decades, confiding only in a military officer whose service he entered.

News of the success of the crew of the *Alkelda* was not forthcoming, and it may be assumed that, if Robinson was a truthful man, the treasure remains hidden to this day. If someone was lucky enough to recover it, they'd find themselves in possession of a fortune, for the treasure would now be worth somewhere in the region of £81,100,000.

♪ The Armada ♪

Thomas Babington Macaulay, 1st Baron Macaulay
Published in *Songs for Sailors*, 1872

Attend, all ye who list to hear our noble England's praise
I tell of the thrice famous deeds she wrought in ancient days,
When that great fleet invincible, against her bore, in vain,
The richest spoils of Mexico, the stoutest hearts of Spain.
It was about the lovely close of a warm summer day,
There came a gallant merchant ship full sail to Plymouth Bay;
Her crew hath seen Castile's black fleet, beyond Aurigny's isle
At earliest twilight, on the waves, lie heaving many a mile.
At sunrise she escaped their van, by God's especial grace;
And the tall *Pinta*, till the noon, had held her close in chase.
Forthwith a guard, at every gun, was placed along the wall;
The beacon blazed upon the roof of Edgecombe's lofty hall;
Many a light fishing bark put out, to pry along the coast;
And with loose reign, and bloody spur, rode inland many a post.
With his white hair, unbonneted, the stout old sheriff comes,
Behind him march the halberdiers, before him sound the drums:
His yeomen, round the market cross, make clear an ample space,
For there behoves him to set up the standard of her grace;
And haughtily the trumpets peal, and gaily dance the bells,
As slow upon the labouring wind the royal blazon swells.
Look how the lion of the sea lifts up his ancient crown,
And underneath his deadly paw treads the gay lilies down!
So stalked he when he turn'd to flight, on that famed Picard field,
Bohemia's plume, and Genoa's bow, and Caesar's eagle shield:
So glared he when, at Agincourt, in wrath he turned to bay,
And crush'd and torn, beneath his claws, the princely hunters lay.
Ho! strike the flagship deep, Sir Knight: ho! scatter flowers, fair maids:
Ho! gunners, fire a loud salute: ho! gallants, draw your blades:
Thou, sun, shine on her joyously; ye breezes, waft her wide;
Our glorious *semper eadem*, the banner of our pride.
The freshening breeze of eve unfurl'd that banner's massy fold,
The parting gleam of sunshine kiss'd that haughty scroll of gold:
Night sank upon the dusky beach, and on the purple sea;
Such night in England ne'er had been, nor e'er again shall be.

From Eddystone to Berwick bounds, from Lynn to Milford bay,
That time of slumber was as bright and busy as the day;
For swift to east, and swift to west, the ghastly war-flame spread,
High on St Michael's Mount it shone, it shone on Beachy Head:
Far on the deep the Spaniard saw, along each southern shire,
Cape beyond the cape, in endless range, those twinkling points of fire.
The fisher left his skiff to rock on Tamar's glittering waves,
The rugged miners poured to war, from Mendip's sunless caves;
O'er Longleat's towers, o'er Cranbourne's oaks, the fiery herald flew,
He roused the shepherds of Stonehenge, the rangers of Beaulieu.
Right sharp and quick the bells all night rang out from Bristol town;
And, ere the day, three hundred horse had met on Clifton Down.
The sentinel on Whitehall gate look'd forth into the night,
And saw, o'erhanging Richmond Hill, the streak of blood-red light:
Then bugle's note, and cannon's roar, the deathlike silence broke,
And with one start, and with one cry, the royal city woke;
At once, on all her stately gates arose the answering fires;
At once the wild alarum clash'd from all her reeling spires;
From all the batteries of the Tower pealed loud the voice of fear,
And all the thousand masts of Thames sent back a louder cheer:
And from the furthest wards was heard the rush of hurrying feet,
And the broad streams of pikes and flags rush'd down each roaring street:
And broader still became the blaze, and louder still the din,
As fast from every village round the horse came spurring in;
And eastward straight, from wild Blackheath the warlike errand went
And roused, in many an ancient hall, the gallant squires of Kent:
Southward, from Surrey's pleasant hills, flew those bright couriers forth;
High on bleak Hampstead's swarthy moor, they started for the north;
And on, and on, without a pause, untired they bounded still;
All night from tower to tower they sprang; they sprang from hill to hill;
Till the proud peak unfurl'd the flag o'er Darwin's rocky dales:
Till, like volcanoes, flared to heaven the stormy hills of Wales;
Till twelve fair counties saw the blaze on Malvern's lonely height;
Till streamed in crimson, on the wind, the Wrekin's crest of light;
Till, broad and fierce, the star came forth, on Ely's stately fane,
And tower and hamlet rose in arms, o'er all the boundless plain;
Till Belvoir's lordly terraces the sign to Lincoln sent,
And Lincoln sped the message on, o'er the wide vale of Trent;
Till Skiddaw saw the fire that burned on Gaunt's embattled pile,
And the red glare on Skiddaw rouse the burghers of Carlisle.

Pieces of Eight

One of England's most memorable naval victories occurred in 1588, when the Spanish Armada, that magnificent fleet of 130 vessels that sailed from Europe with the sole intention of seizing Queen Elizabeth I's crown, was defeated. About half of the enemy's ships were wrecked at various points around the coast of the British Isles, where they lay forgotten for more than 300 years.

Then, in the summer of 1905, a team of divers claimed to have made a remarkable discovery off the shore of Tobermory on the Isle of Mull: they'd found and reached the so-called *Admiral of Florence*, a mysterious foreign galleon that had been buried in the sand for generations. This legendary wreck was thought to have played a part in the failed invasion attempt three centuries earlier; and though there was no possibility of raising her, she and her sunken treasures were gifted to the Earl of Argyll in 1641 by King Charles I. Since then, a great many recovery attempts had been made, and certain artefacts, such as anchors, plates and a silver bell, were found, but there was never any sign of the vast riches that were thought to have been on board.

In 1901, a handful of American newspapers began boasting that a trio of men from Philadelphia had succeeded in reaching the wreck and had snatched all of its glistening fortunes from under the noses of the then Duke of Argyll and the British Government. These amateur bounty hunters allegedly returned home as millionaires, leaving the duke's coffers empty. In response, the duke began to prepare a deep-sea diving mission of his own to find out whether or not these alarming rumours were true.

His team of divers finally reached the wreck on 1 August 1905, and they returned to the surface with five pieces of eight, silver Spanish coins that were thought to be worth a pretty penny. The money had been found inside the hulk of the *Admiral of Florence*, and a handful of other items, such as silver candlesticks and gold-plated ornaments, were also recovered … but there was no sign of the promised horde of treasure. Could the American rumours have been true after all, or was this Spanish galleon never laden with gold in the first place? These questions were never answered, but the present duke continues scouring the seabed of Tobermory to this day, just in case.

The Recovery of the Crown Jewels from the Wash

King John, the infamous monarch who succeeded Richard the Lionheart, sat on the English throne from 1199 to 1216. Though he's often remembered by history as a tyrant and popularized in the story of Robin Hood, his name is also linked to another well-known legend: the time when the Crown Jewels of England were lost forever in the sea.

It was 1216, the year after John had added his seal to the Magna Carta. The country was in a state of political turmoil. The French Prince Louis had sent an army to invade the south of England at the request of some of the rebellious English barons who longed to see the back of their sovereign. King John retreated to King's Lynn, Norfolk, where he contracted dysentery on 10 October, and his health deteriorated quickly. With Louis' forces firmly established in the south, it wasn't safe for the ailing monarch to journey to Windsor or London; instead he decided to head north to Lincolnshire, and the quickest route was across the sands of the Wash, which became navigable during low tide.

On the twelfth of the month the king and his mile-long cavalcade set off for Wisbech, where the water was relatively easy to cross. With horses and wagons leading the procession, the company began their perilous trek across the 2-mile stretch of boggy marshland. Though the king and his knights had reached the other side without any difficulty, the royal treasure train travelled slower than the incoming tide, and was eventually overtaken by the water. All the sovereign could do was watch helplessly as his wagonload of priceless artefacts was washed away and lost in Norfolk's quicksand.

Ever since that day, treasure seekers have tried in vain to find this missing horde of gold. Efforts were renewed in the Edwardian era, when the Society of Antiquarians announced their intention to search for the medieval Crown Jewels. The society's secretary, William St John Hope, had long been engaged in a study of the tides to determine the exact time the wagon would have been crossing the sand, and by early April 1906, he was confident he'd located the precise spot where it vanished. This area, he believed, was no longer a bog, but now a piece of dry land on a private estate close to Sutton Bridge, near the Welland River. By his calculations, the treasure hadn't been washed away by the sea, as many others had speculated, but had in fact become buried some 40ft underneath the stratum of silt.

By the end of April, a new clue came to light when a local publican from Wisbech came forward. He'd heard about Mr Hope's project, and believed he may have once found a piece of the treasure. In the winter of 1905, he'd been digging for clams on the sandbanks at Gedney Drove End, a hamlet built on the old marshlands on the fringe of the Wash, and unearthed a mud-encrusted goblet. He took it back to his house, and assuming it had no value, placed it with some old timber and forgot all about it. Some months later, a builder was carrying out some repairs at the publican's home when he spotted the old goblet. Thinking it an interesting curiosity, he offered the publican a shilling for it, which was gratefully accepted.

The builder took the goblet home and began cleaning it. It soon became apparent that the item was made of silver, and was beautifully ornamented. He showed it to a jeweller, who, to the builder's surprise, offered a considerable sum for it. The builder refused.

In light of this new information an investigation was launched. The cup was located and its owner consented for it to be examined and restored. A date of 1162 was found engraved on the side of the vessel, along with a lion's head and various scroll-like designs. The goblet, which was presumed to have been a communal cup, stood about 8ins high and weighed a little less than 3lb. Investigators concluded that it probably formed part of King John's lost treasure. The question was: where was the rest?

Though searches continued for many years, there were no more discoveries. In 1932, a new company, the Fen Research Company Limited, was formed with the sole intention of recovering the fortune. The directors persuaded various Lincolnshire landlords to allow their estates to be excavated. Despite procuring a set of expensive electrical divination rods, which the directors believed would be able to detect the presence of precious metals under the ground, surprisingly little was found.

Just two years later, a startling new theory came to light, which threatened to bring all such searches to a grinding and disappointing halt. Following some investigative work, Reverend Oscar Reginald Plant, the rector of Rockingham, Northamptonshire, concluded that the majority of the Crown Jewels hadn't been lost in the Wash after all, for they had been hidden by the king prior to his journey north. The rector's research revealed that the king had stayed at Rockingham Castle just days before the disaster. In fact, this 'Windsor Castle of the Midlands' was one of King John's favourite residences, owing to its extensive hunting grounds. The rector had been scouring the castle's archives and found a collection of old inventories, which suggested that most of the treasure hadn't even been in the luggage wagon when it was washed away, yet a vast collection of riches arrived at Rockingham with the king.

Though some royal treasure chests were still in the castle, they were empty; the records indicated that the contents had been removed shortly before the king left for Lincolnshire, but it wasn't clear exactly where they'd been placed. All the rector was sure about was that they weren't in the luggage wagon. He didn't believe the king would have entrusted all his riches to his courtiers, who could have rebelled at any moment, just like the barons. The rector theorized that King John knew he was seriously ill and didn't want to risk his treasure falling into the hands of the invading French enemy, so he concealed it somewhere near Rockingham Castle, the place he loved so dearly.

The cleric began searching the land between the castle and his rectory, and found a false wall inside the vaults of his church. Behind this were silver plates and a silver chalice, dated 1570. Whilst this clearly hadn't formed part of King John's treasure, this discovery confirmed that Rockingham was indeed a perfect hiding place. These silver Holy Communion vessels, which had once been used by the sovereigns of England, were said to have been worth £4,000, or approximately £1,190,000 today.

Rockingham Castle was built on a maze of subterranean passages, and though the rector proceeded to search every inch of the building, he was a cripple, and was eventually forced to admit defeat. He died none the wiser in 1956, and his theory was largely forgotten.

♪ The Sailor's Friend ♪

Printed in *The Shetland Times*, 8 February 1875

Britain's toiling sons arise,
Now the struggle is at hand,
Drop the screen from off your eyes,
Cast the stigma from your land,
Let the greedy ones be told
You your efforts now will lend,
Not to them who thirst for gold,
But to aid the sailor's friend.

He, who by himself hath stood
Every taunt from Mammon's store –
He, who stems the angry flood
Breaking forth with dreadful roar;
Lion-hearted, dauntless he
Will the sailor's grievance rend,
Smooth his passage o'er the sea –
Plimsoll is the sailor's friend.

Let the movement onward press,
With the avalanche's roar;
May the sound – Redress! Redress!
Now be heard from shore to shore;
Look upon the orphan's tear,
Let its eye to pity lend –
Lord and Commons give an ear,
Listen to the sailor's friend.

Widows may not cease to mourn,
Orphans yet may wail and weep,
Lov'd ones may from them be borne
'Neath the stormy wave to sleep;
But the greedy thirst for gain
Should not those sorrow tend;
Britons look upon the sailors slain,
Aid and help the sailor's friend.

Lost Underwater Cities

In 1949, a world-class Grecian diver named Johannes Rodittis stunned the world when he announced that he'd discovered not one but three abandoned cities underneath the Mediterranean Sea, lying between Sicily and Tunisia. During a diving expedition he took great delight in visiting the aquatic ruins, which had seemingly lain undisturbed since the time of the ancients.

Approximately 70ft below the surface of the waves could be found roads and remarkably well-preserved buildings, protected all those years by veils of shells and seaweeds; and among the corals were some fine ancient sculptures.

The diver returned laden with samples of earthenware vases, as well as small statuettes; and scientists concluded that the submarine settlements were probably constructed in about 1000 BC, before a devastating earthquake caused the land to sink into the ocean.

An Underwater Observatory

According to a report from Marseilles, printed in *The Derby Daily Telegraph* on 19 June 1883, a gentleman named Monsieur Toselli succeeded in building a wondrous new underwater observatory that would transport up to eight passengers at any one time to the depths of the Mediterranean Sea. It was constructed from glass, steel and bronze, and was capable of resisting the pressure of the ocean at a depth of up to 120 metres. The structure had a glass bottom, allowing the travellers to observe the wonders of the seabed. A gigantic waterproof lamp provided ample lighting, and an onboard telephone permitted the tourists to communicate with their friends on the shore, describing to them the many mysteries of the ocean.

♪ Address to Some Beautiful Sea-Shells Left by the Tide ♪

J.H.R. Bayley
Printed in the *Gloucester Journal*, 18 November 1843

Hail! bright shells of an ocean home!
Freshly borne through light and foam:
Hail! to your sea-tone, wild and free –
As music's fairy strain should be!
Your wave-worn crust, and purple curl,
Rival the ruby, and vie with the pearl.
There's lustre in each conch-curved aisle,
As rich as the light of beauty's smile:
And wonders ye are, come how ye may,
In the breaker's whirl, or the wavelet's spray.

Are ye the homes were the Nereid dwells,
Or have Tritons sported in your cells?
Say, were ye washed from the merman's halls,
Crystal grots, or coral walls?
Have ye been where the grampus rolled,
Or icebergs shone like burning gold?
Sprung ye from enchanted caves,
Fathoms below the noisy waves?
Or kept ye watch in the sunless deep,
Where the wrecked ones slept their lasting sleep?

No matter! the office ye've held, or where –
Heaven formed you, and pronounced you fair!
Had ye clung to the jewel or gem,
What brighter had been your gleam through them?
And the mellow tread of sea-nymphs' feet
Were vain to make your song more sweet.
Beautiful shells of the dark blue wave!
Floating o'er shingles, or flushing in cave –
Ye're the fairest in form, and the purest in tone,
That Neptune may boast of, or Ocean may own!

Under the Channel to France

On 9 December 1859, the *Dundee, Perth and Cupar Advertiser* discussed a foreign proposal 'to make a submarine tunnel from Dover to Calais'. Though this sounded like a fabulous idea to merchants and travellers, the Napoleonic Wars were still within living memory, having come to an end in 1815 with the defeat of the French army at Waterloo; and the people of Britain feared that there was always a chance that France's current emperor, Napoleon III, could 'make way for one less friendly'. Though there were concerns that such a tunnel would prove useful to any enemies who were plotting to invade this *sceptred isle*, it was questionable whether or not science could ever achieve such an ambitious feat of engineering, anyway.

This wasn't the first time such a tunnel was proposed. The idea was first mooted in about 1802; and on 22 January 1825, a letter was printed in *The Morning Post* citing an earlier article outlining the possibilities of excavation.

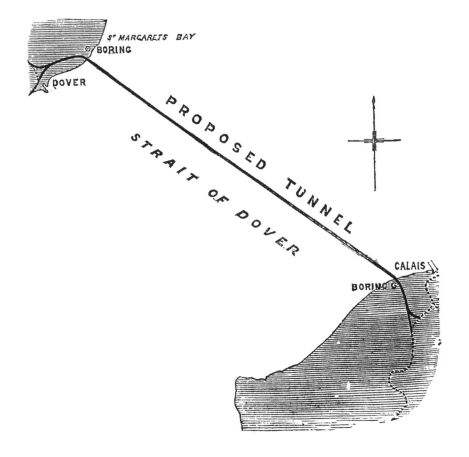

'It meets my most decided approbation,' declared the correspondent, known simply as *An Englishman*. 'The [company in charge of overseeing the work] will undoubtedly derive immense annual revenues from the tolls, and receive the benedictions of travellers from all countries, while passing through such an easy and direct communication.'

The idea wasn't forgotten, and throughout the century it was perpetually tweaked and deliberated. In 1846, an estimated cost of the project was placed at about £8,000,000, the equivalent of about £24,060,000,000 in today's currency. This was a huge investment; and two years later, a Frenchman proposed a cheaper and simpler alternative to the French Academy of Sciences. He believed that a floating tunnel could be placed on top of the waves, through which telegraph cables and steam locomotives could run, but his idea was soon scrapped.

The pros and cons of a tunnel under the English Channel were debated until 1866, when a French newspaper, *Le Propagateur*, reported that surveys at Calais had begun at last, and huts were erected for the use of engineers. It was finally concluded that owing to the turbulent nature of the narrow strait between Dover and Calais, an underground railway link would make journeys to and from the Continent much more convenient, especially for travellers who suffered seasickness.

The map on the previous page, showing the planned route, dates back to the mid-1870s. The tunnel was to be bored through a deep undersea bed of chalk, and a double line of rails would enable regular trains to run between Dover and Calais. The entrances to the tunnel, both in England and France, would be well guarded, and would begin at a considerable distance from the shore. The depth of water over the proposed line wasn't considered an obstacle, for nowhere did it exceed 180ft. In fact, it was said that if Westminster Abbey could be sunk in the deepest part of the Channel, the top 45ft of its towers would stick out of the water.

It seemed that after decades of dreaming and planning, the ambitious aspirations of two great nations were finally being realized. The only remaining challenge was securing enough funding to complete the work.

'I believe, as Stephenson jocularly said of a railway to the moon, it is only a question of expense,' said a journalist for *The Cornish Times*, writing on 26 May 1866. 'The tunnel is not likely to be made in the time of the youngest now alive.'

Indeed, it took more than a century for the project to be finished. The 31.4-mile-long Channel Tunnel was triumphantly opened in 1994, having cost, according to Eurotunnel's website, £9,000,000,000.

Railways at the Bottom of the Sea

In the 1870s, newspapers and gossip columns were brimming with speculation that the construction of a magnificent railway tunnel beneath the English Channel could be imminent. However, in 1875, a Parisian inventor named Dr Jean Marie Auguste Lacomme claimed that such a structure was an unnecessary expense, for he'd designed a submarine railway carriage that travelled directly through the water.

The hermetically sealed carriages were made of galvanized iron. To prevent the train from floating, the carriages were attached to a heavy eight-wheeled truck, which ran on a line of rails that was laid directly on the ocean bed. In the event of an accident or emergency, the carriages could be detached, allowing them to rise to the surface.

Critics were quick to point out that it would have been practically unthinkable to burn coal underwater, but the inventor explained that his submarine engine could be driven by compressed air. In fact, an enormous quantity of breathable air was to be distributed throughout the train via a network of pipes. Onboard electric lights illuminated both the track and the interior of the vessel, and the entrance for the passengers was sealed tightly when all were aboard. In addition, strong glass windows were provided throughout the entirety of the train, making this undersea vehicle one of the most scenic modes of transport never to be constructed.

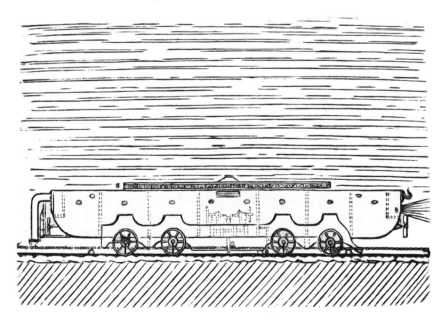

♪ The Sea Cave: Song of the Sea Nymph ♪

John Tate
Printed in *The Bury Times*, 8 August 1857

Ah! who is so free
As the nymph of the sea,
As I sit in my crystal cave, –
Binding up my curls
With the ocean pearls,
And the gems of the deep sea wave?

Early in the morn,
By old Triton's horn,
I am waked from a magic spell;
And all the day long
I am charmed with the song
Of the mermaids around my cell.

All flow'rets sweet
Are springing at my feet
As I pace the bright waves under;
They care not to shun
The illimitable sun,
Nor shrink at the booming thunder.

My pastime I take
With the huge sea snake,
As he glides through the foaming wave:
And the dolphin bold,
With his coat of gold,
Is a guest in my bright sea cave.

I have many a lark
With the white-tooth'd shark,
As I ride on the dragon's tail. –
It's a fav'rite sport
In this cool resort
To dance on the back of the whale.

On a coral bed
I recline my head,
Down below in the secret deep:-
And the murm'ring sound
Of the billows around
Is sweet to my ear as I sleep.

And sometimes I take,
(For the novelty's sake)
A plunge in the maelstrom wild;
And the furies bow
As adown I go,
For they rev'rence the ocean child.

But I may not tell
What a dismal hell
Of demons inhabit beneath. –
Pale, pale grows the face
That looks down to that place,
O'ershadow'd by the wings of death.

What Fishermen Found

One day in 1850, a fisherman trawling the coast of France made a seemingly ground-breaking discovery. Instead of fish, in his net he found an incredibly long piece of seaweed, so lengthy, in fact, that he couldn't find either end of it, no matter how hard he pulled and tugged. He took his knife and cut off a portion of the weed, only to find its centre was filled with gold. This was an extraordinarily rare find indeed! He took his prize catch straight to Boulogne, only to learn that his piece of golden seaweed was actually a portion of the first telegraph cable to have been laid between Britain and mainland Europe. Fortunately, the cable wasn't in use at the time, and a new fully functional replacement was laid the following year.

In the 1920s, a travelling fair began making its way across Britain, stopping at a variety of destinations to delight the local townsfolk with exotic foods, fairground rides, amusement shows and wondrous exhibits. The fair arrived at Burnley, Lancashire, on 12 July 1928, where it remained for three days. One of its attractions was billed as 'the lobster-clawed girl', a true mystery of the deep. The girl's name was Sealina, and her exhibitor was a Grimsby fisherman who claimed to have caught this unusual sea-dwelling creature on one of his fishing expeditions. He took her ashore, tidied her up, and seizing a lucrative opportunity, promptly joined the travelling fair. The public's interest was sparked when advertisements for this curious new attraction appeared in the local press. She was said to possess remarkable intelligence and resembled an ordinary young woman, except for her hands.

Despite the fisherman's bold claims, modern medical experts would probably be of the opinion that Sealina was just an ordinary girl with a rare congenital condition known as ectrodactyly, or 'lobster-claw syndrome', which prevented the ordinary development of her hands.

Other fairground attractions that were paraded in front of paying crowds in the 1920s included Chief Niambi, 'the wild dancing bushman'; 23in-tall Little Nobbler, the smallest horse in the world; and Tiny Tim, a 40-year-old man from Southport who stood the same height as the horse. Despite being half the size of a Maxim gun, Mr Tim was thrice called upon by military authorities during the First World War and asked to enlist. He failed his medical inspection on each occasion.

The Capture of a Sea Serpent

Terrifying tales of sea serpents and underwater monsters lurking in the deepest parts of the ocean, ready to drag down passing ships with their enormous tentacles, have pervaded mankind's myths and legends since time immemorial. Over the centuries, the pages of history books have been filled with eyewitness accounts describing the unidentified creatures people had allegedly seen for themselves. In 1827, for instance, reports came flooding in from Norway from dozens of people who believed they'd spotted a gigantic sea serpent frolicking in the ocean. According to *The Staffordshire Advertiser*, it was '500 feet long' with a body 'about the thickness of a hogshead'. So convincing were these claims that the authorities offered £25 to anyone brave enough – or perhaps lucky enough – to capture the beast. Nobody succeeded; but fifty years later, a monstrous sea serpent was captured off the shores of Oban, Scotland, in the spring of 1877.

'About four o'clock on Tuesday, an animal or fish, evidently of gigantic size, was seen sporting in the bay near Heather Island,' said a reporter for *The Daily Gazette for Middlesbrough* on 2 May. 'Its appearance evidently perplexed a large number of spectators assembled on the pier, and several telescopes were directed towards it. A careful look satisfied us that it was of the serpent species, it carrying its head full 25 feet above the water.'

A number of boats were launched, armed with an assortment of nets and weapons. After a long and frantic struggle the monster was lassoed. It took the efforts of seventy of the town's strongest men to heave it ashore, where a team of marine biologists carefully examined its body.

'The extreme length is 101ft, and the thickest part is about 25ft from the head, which is 11ft in circumference,' the newspaper report continued. 'At this part is fixed a pair of fins, which are 4ft long by nearly 7ft across the side. Further back is a long dorsal fin, extending for at least 12 or 13ft, and 5ft high in front, tapering to 1ft. The tail is more of a flattened termination to the body proper than anything else. The eyes are very small in proportion and elongated, and gills of the length of 2.5ft behind. There are no external ears; and as Dr Campbell did not wish the animal handled till he communicated with some eminent scientific gentleman, we could not ascertain if there were teeth or not.'

The same story was featured in dozens of other local and national newspapers, all of them asserting the same fact: this unidentified creature was roughly the same length as a blue whale, the largest known marine mammal in existence. So, what exactly could the creature have been? The answer to this question was never disclosed to the public.

♪ Sea-Shells ♪

Printed in the *Hereford Journal*, 1 August 1849

Far out at sea, a fairy boat
Has set her tiny sail,
And, swiftly, see it onward float,
As freshens still the gale.
A rainbow in it must have slept,
To give it tints so fair;
Or loveliest angel in it wept,
A pearl in every tear:
More bright than pen of mine can tell,
Sailed on that little fearless shell.

Deep in the chambers of the sea,
Where Ocean's mermaids dwell,
A palace stood; it seemed to me,
Its every stone a shell:
And oh! what glorious hues were they
That struck upon my eye,
Of blue, and green, of gold, and grey,
That there unnoticed lie:
As violets sweet, in loveliest dells,
So blush unseen these beauteous shells.

Thus, on the sea, and 'neath its waves,
These painted sea-gems lie,
As tomb-stones o'er the many graves
Of low-born men and high;
And when they rest upon the shore,
In wealth's luxurious ease,
They sound to us the solemn roar
They learned beneath the seas:
As exiles, though afar they roam,
Still sing the songs they learned at home.

The Mermaid who Lived on Land

Naval historians widely agree that the legend of mermaids is more than 3,000 years old, and originated in Ancient Assyria. From this Middle Eastern land the folktale spread around the world, first reaching the shores of England during Saxon times. Ever since then, sailors and landlubbers alike have fallen in love with tales of beautiful sea-dwelling creatures that are half women, half fish.

Though the majority of people appreciated that these were nothing more than charming fairy stories, there were some who insisted there must have been a speck of truth behind the legend. In fact, reported sightings of merfolk have been frequent, the most notable, perhaps, being made by Christopher Columbus, who claimed to have spotted three mermaids rising out of the sea in 1493. Rational thinkers attributed these sightings to manatees, which often float upright in the water when nursing their young.

Some years earlier, in 1403, there was a report of a mermaid being caught off the coast of Holland, then brought to land and tamed. According to *The Yorkshire Post and Leeds Intelligencer*, 'some milkmaids caught a strange creature, half woman, half fish, during a flood.' She was taken to the town hall, where she was provided with lodgings and a private tutor who lived with her and educated her.

'She learnt to spin and show devotion at prayer,' the article went on to explain; 'she would laugh, and when women came into the Town-house to spin with her for diversion, she would signify by signs she knew their meaning in some sort, though she could never be taught to speak.'

It was said that the human half of this mermaid could live and breathe perfectly well in the open air, but her tail was constantly kept in a tub of water. She lived for sixteen years, and when she died she was purportedly buried in a churchyard in Haarlem.

Incredibly, this wasn't the only documented domestic 'mermaid'. In 1925, reports from the island of Flores, of the Azores, spoke of the taming of not one but two live mermaids by a local hotelkeeper. These amazing creatures became somewhat of a local attraction, and each night they could be seen frolicking in the bay. More and more people heard about the spectacle, and in no time at all huge crowds of visitors came flocking to see for themselves. The mermaids became so popular that the hotelkeeper made a small fortune, and built an even bigger hotel to accommodate the growing number of guests.

Sadly for him, his moneymaking venture came to an abrupt end in 1930, when a new police commissioner was appointed; and he didn't believe in mermaids. One night he took a boat out into the bay, where he caught the hotelkeeper's two daughters swimming around. Their faces were caked in white make-up and prosthetic tails had been fitted over their legs.

The Mystery of the Japanese Sea-Diver

On 12 September 1874, the national papers told how the people of Portrush in Northern Ireland were 'thrown into a state of alarm' by the appearance of a previously unheard-of species of sea monster. The London paper, *The Daily News*, explained that a 'scientific and highly-gifted naturalist' named Dr Snaggleton had taken a boat out to sea, when his attention was drawn to a most extraordinary creature standing on the top of a small cliff.

'In form and colour he had much the appearance of an ordinary man,' said the doctor; 'the skin was perfectly white, with the exception of the lower part of the body, which appeared to be stripped and of a blue and white colour. There was a great quantity of black hair underneath the chin, and the nose appeared to be prominent and well developed.'

Then, according to the paper, the 'merman' suddenly took a side leap into the sea, landing within 20ft of the boat, and never reappeared.

The doctor concluded that the creature probably belonged to a rare species known as *Submergis Japanarius*, or 'Japanese sea-diver', which had only ever before been sighted on the northern shores of Japan. According to his research, these creatures congregated in small shoals near Yokohama, and when on land, were commonly mistaken for humans. How one ended up in Northern Ireland, the doctor couldn't explain, but it was his intention to capture a specimen one day and exhibit it in Belfast Museum. The museum curators must have been sorely disappointed when Dr Snaggleton died before he'd completed his fantastical mission.

♪ A Song of the Sea Fairies ♪

Lord Thurlow
Printed in *The Chester Courant*, 14 March 1815

We tread upon the golden sand,
When the waves are rolling in,
And the Porpus comes to land,
And to leap he doth begin,
Snorting to the fishy air:
Prepare, prepare,
Good Housewives, keep your fires bright,
For your Mates come home to-night.

Now the drenched nets are drawn
From the swaying of the seas:
'Faith, your rings must go to pawn,
Blow such bitter winds as these,
The moon, the moon,
Riding at her highest noon,
Swells the orbed waters bright,
And your Mates come home to-night,

Through our crisped locks the wind,
Like a sighing lover, plays:
Now let Joan, and Alice kind,
Make the wint'ry faggot blaze;
And the pot be Lucy's care:
Prepare, prepare,
And see you speed your welcome right,
For your Mates come home to-night.

Else we'll pinch you black and blue,
Underneath pale Hecate's team;
And the cramp your joints shall rue,
And the night-mare in your dream:
Be sure, be sure,
This, and more you shall endure,
If you smile not, chaste and bright,
When your Mates come home to-night.

Phantom Ships

Legends of phantom ships – vessels with no living crew members on board – have haunted maritime folklore since at least the 1640s. The Age of Sail was in full flow: international trading ships beleaguered the high seas, and the most powerful nations built fleets of warships to defend their lands and conquer their enemies.

South America's Cape Horn and South Africa's Cape of Good Hope were two headlands where phantom ships were frequently spotted. In fact, the latter was where the *Flying Dutchman*, perhaps the most famous spectral ship of all, was often sighted during stormy weather. Legend tells that a Dutch captain, battling against a terrible gale, swore an oath that he'd keep trying to get his ship to harbour rather than surrender to the storm, even if it took him until Judgement Day. He was taken at his word, and sightings of the *Flying Dutchman* have been reported in the region ever since, often suspended in the air just below the horizon. This, scientists claimed, was simply an illusion, caused by the unequal refraction of light, and had nothing at all to do with the paranormal.

Be that as it may, over the decades there have been several notable sightings of this phantom vessel. In the logbook of HMS *Bacchante*, a Royal Navy corvette, is written '*Flying Dutchman* crossed our bows'. This apparently happened on 11 July 1881, during a round the world voyage; and to add credibility to the claim, two of Queen Victoria's grandsons, Princes Albert and George (the future King George V), were serving as midshipmen at the time.

One of the earliest known sightings of a phantom ship occurred in June 1647. The previous January, a vessel had left New Haven, Connecticut, on her maiden voyage, but she was never heard of again ... until the following springtime. It was just before sunset, after a terrible storm had passed, and locals taking an evening stroll were thrilled when they spotted the familiar sails returning to New Haven, when all hope had been lost. They dashed to the banks of the river to get a closer look and to wave at the returning crewmen, only to find that the ship was inexplicably sailing against the wind. How could that be? They continued to watch the curious spectacle until the ship faded away before their eyes and disappeared into thin air.

The poet Henry Wadsworth Longfellow commemorated the curious sighting in verse:

> On she came, with a cloud of canvas,
> Right against the winds that blew;
> Until the eye could distinguish
> The faces of the crew.
>
> And the masts, with all their rigging,
> Fell slowly, one by one,
> And the hulk dilated and vanished
> As a sea-mist in the sun.

Sightings of a ghostly shipwreck at Cape Horn have prevailed for centuries. The vessel is said to be completely derelict: its sails are tattered and its decks awash with the sea. Logical thinkers have put the vision down to ship-like shapes of jagged rocks situated close to the headland, but the illusion has seemed real enough to draw many a vessel and their crew to a watery grave.

On a certain day each year, a phantom ship is alleged to appear off Cap d'Espoir, Gaspé Bay, Quebec. She is said to be illuminated by artificial lighting, and scores of men crowd her deck. One of the officers stands at the foot of the bowsprit, facing the shore, with a female figure clinging on to his arm. The lights are eventually extinguished as the vessel sinks beneath the waves. She is supposed to be the ghost of a British flagship, whose fleet was sent out by Queen Anne during the eighteenth century to attack the French forts in the region; but the ship and all hands aboard were lost.

The eighteenth-century packet boat *Light* was wrecked in close proximity to the place where RMS *Titanic* went down on 15 April 1912. Witnesses passing the scene of the accident claim that whenever a storm is threatened, a ball of fire emerges from out of the sea and transforms into the shape of the *Light*. It floats on the surface of the water for a brief moment before sinking back into the ocean again.

According to a correspondent of the *Daily Dispatch*, several men aboard a British destroyer witnessed a remarkable yet unexplainable sight in 1916, during the First World War. It was dusk, and in the distance the crew spotted a luminous warship. It came towards them at a terrific speed, and as it drew nearer the sailors descried that the vessel was red-hot, and that there wasn't a single soul on board. It would have collided with the destroyer, had it not been for the quick-thinking captain, who managed to avert disaster.

'It was an extremely uncanny spectacle,' said one of the sailors, 'and one I shall never forget, even if I live to be a thousand years old. It shot past us. We watched it disappear in the distance, but what came of it we do not know.'

A different kind of phantom ship materialized in Falkirk in 1925, when a confidence trickster named George Milne Porter convinced several local tradesmen that he was a commercial traveller. He claimed to have been importing a large quantity of smuggled goods into Cardiff on board a vessel named SS *Phantom*, which was due to arrive imminently. He promised the tradesmen a good deal on tea, sugar, coffee, cigarettes, whisky, brandy, crêpe de chine, Japanese silk, cloth and fur, providing they paid in cash up front. The tradesmen couldn't resist, and each placed large orders to the combined sum of £500. The alluded ship, however, lived up to her name and vanished into thin air, along with Porter and the cash.

The Cornish Goblin Ship

For centuries, the waters off the coast of Cornwall have been visited by a unique type of vessel, the likes of which have never been seen anywhere else in the world. She has been dubbed the 'goblin ship', and not only sails the sea, but also travels a good distance inland as well. According to eyewitnesses, this spectre appears at the seaside village of Porthcurno, some 9 or 10 miles from Penzance. She is a black, square-rigged, single-masted ship, which sometimes appears to be towing a small boat behind her. No crew member has ever been sighted on deck, but despite having no living captain, she's said to glide steadily through the waves and doesn't stop when she reaches land: she carries on a steady course over the golden beach just as easily as if she was on water. She continues for about half a mile before vanishing like a puff of smoke.

Interestingly, this region of Cornwall was once home to Madgy Figgy, a black-hearted witch who used to sit on the cliffs and summon up storms whenever merchant seamen were returning with cargo-laden vessels. If the ships were wrecked and the sailors drowned, Figgy would claim the goods for herself.

♪ The Sailor Boy's Grave ♪

Printed in *Berrow's Worcester Journal*, 22 September 1855

Bright, bright were the sailor boy's dreams in life's morning,
When hope with its fairy-forms gilded the way,
And a thousand sweet visions of happiness dawning,
Were spreading their shadows throughout the long day.
Quick, quick beats his heart, at the buoyant bark's motion,
For his childhood's first dream – his first love –
Were the foam-crested waves of the wide-spreading ocean,
With the sun and the sea-bird above.

Soon, soon were his hopes and fairy-dreams banish'd;
Not long did they gladden his sight;
For he sickened, and quickly the light of life vanish'd,
Till it wan'd into death's gloomy night.
They buried him then in the shroud they had made him,
'Neath his childhood's first dream – his first love –
And sea-shells are scattered around where they laid him,
With the sun and the sea-bird above.

No flowers bloom in beauty; no stone tells his story;
No dirge, save the wind and the wave;
No tablet of fame, and no emblem of glory,
Are found near the sailor-boy's grave.
Yet his head rests in peace on his coral-rock pillow,
'Neath his childhood's first dream – his first love –
And the sun and sea-bird, and foam-crested billow,
All sparkle in splendor above.

The Ghost of a Murdered Sailor

An old Portsmouth legend tells of a gruesome murder, which occurred in the Blue Posts coaching house in the early 1700s. The story goes that one night a cold and weary sailor entered the inn and requested a room. Before turning in, he sat by the fireplace and warmed himself with copious amounts of rum. During the evening, as he grew progressively merrier and his tongue became increasingly loose, he began bragging that his bag contained a vast quantity of money and jewels. Whether that was true or simply a drunken boast, nobody can be sure, but what is certain is that when the sailor went upstairs to bed he was followed by a stranger who tried to snatch his bag. A scuffle broke out, and the sailor's throat was slashed. The murderer fled into the night and never returned.

The next morning, the landlady discovered the mariner's body lying in a pool of blood at the foot of his bed. She tied an old scarf around his neck, and not wanting to attract any bad publicity, she and her son buried the corpse in the back yard, swearing an oath that they'd never utter a word of this to another living soul.

Some nights later, another traveller came to the inn and was given the same room as the unfortunate victim. The following day, he angrily asked why the landlady had allowed another man to sleep in the vacant bed in his room without his consent. Perplexed, she insisted that he was the only person to occupy the room, but the traveller was adamant that a white-faced, ill-looking sailor with a blood-red scarf round his neck had spent the whole night in the bed beside him. Recognizing the description of this ghostly sailor, the landlady confessed everything.

Though the Blue Posts was burned to the ground in 1870, the exact spot where the sailor was buried was identified in the 1930s, and a tombstone was erected in his memory in August 1936.

The Devil's Sailor

On the morning of 10 April 1927, the bodies of a Norwegian sea captain and four of his crewmen were discovered on the beach at Bude, a Cornish seaside resort. They'd been washed ashore when their cargo vessel, *Verdanne*, had foundered, but it was thought that they were all still alive when they landed. They cried out for help but nobody came.

During the previous night, a farmer's wife, who lived by the beach, heard a terrible wailing coming from the shore, as if someone was crying for help. It was such an otherworldly sound that she was too afraid to even poke a lantern outside the door, so she did nothing. Her husband assured her it was probably just the wind howling among the rocks and crevices; either that or it was the Devil's Sailor.

This was a terrifying tale that had been handed down in Cornwall for generations. It was said that hundreds of years ago, a sailor tried in vain to flee from the Devil. Unable to outrun his pursuer, he attempted to commit suicide by throwing himself overboard. The Devil was greatly angered by this. As punishment, he washed the sailor ashore before he drowned and chained him in a cave close to the beach of Bude, with the promise that freedom would be his once he'd made a rope of sand. Of course, the sailor was unable to perform such a task, and he died trying. His soul has supposedly haunted the cave ever since; and sometimes his groans have been heard so clearly in the dead of night that superstitious residents have refused to leave their homes after the stroke of midnight. Occasionally, when the full moon was high, his ghost has been seen wandering around the beach in search of a means of making his impossible rope.

Perhaps the lives of the Norwegian sailors could have been spared had it not been for this obscure maritime superstition that originated in the Dark Ages but was still very much feared by the local population.

♪ O The Wild, Wild Winds have Voices ♪

William Cox Bennett
Published in *Songs for Sailors*, 1872

O the wild, wild winds have voices
That only that wife can hear;
One voice that wife rejoices,
While one but speaks of fear.
As she listens, the winds moan by,
And they tell of a prayed–for ship,
Of the look from a longed–for eye,
And the sound from a long-lost lip.

Now what does she hear them tell,
As, without, through the night they sweep?
Of his whaler speeding well
Home – home'er a waveless deep;
Yes, she hears in the winds a voice
That's telling how swift his ship
Speeds on, her heart to rejoice
With a kiss from his longed–for lip.

Now what do the wild gusts utter,
As, by, the night–winds moan?
Of tempest and wreck they mutter,
Of peril and death alone;
Of a bare hull swept before
The storm – of a foundering ship –
Of a face she shall see no more,
And a vainly longed–for lip.

A Haunted Ship and a Gruesome Murder

On Sunday, 28 February 1864, the British cargo ship *Pontiac* arrived at the Port of Leith, Edinburgh. Dockworkers helping to moor the ship would never have suspected that all was not well below deck. Little did they know that in the bowels of the vessel a vicious crewman was clapped in irons, accused of murdering a shipmate in cold blood and seriously wounding another.

The police were summoned as soon as the captain came ashore. Two constables were sent to arrest the prisoner and take him to the police station, where he and several witnesses were questioned, and details of the whole sorry affair began to unravel.

The suspect was a Greek sailor named Jean Moyatos, who spoke very little English. He'd joined the ship at Valparaíso, Chile, the previous July. From there, the ship began her voyage north to Callao, Peru, where she was due to collect a cargo of guano. With everything safely stowed on board, the *Pontiac* began her return journey to Britain; but in the afternoon of 13 October, long before the English coast had come into view, something terrible occurred: Moyatos plunged a knife into two of his fellow seamen, seemingly without motive. The men had been off duty, resting in their bunks, when the attack took place. One of the victims, Robert Campbell, died from his injuries; the other, George Williams, was dangerously wounded, but the ship's surgeon expected him to recover.

Why Moyatos had committed such a vile act, nobody could be sure; all that was certain was that two nights earlier, something inexplicable took place on board the *Pontiac*. The mate and the steersman were standing alone at the helm when the latter spotted something odd.

'Who's that by the cabin door?' said the steersman.

The mate looked towards where his colleague was pointing but saw nothing, for there were no other crew members on the quarterdeck at the time. The steersman, however, was quite convinced that someone was lurking, watching their every move.

'There he is again, standing by the captain's window!' he insisted, and proceeded to describe the strange-looking man quite eloquently.

Though the mate was convinced that the steersman must have been hallucinating, he went to investigate. He searched every inch of the deck, but found no one.

The following night, a cabin boy, who'd heard about the steersman's encounter, became convinced that an evil presence was nearby. He was so frightened that his cries awoke all the other sleeping seamen. They tried to comfort the terrified young lad, but he was certain he'd sensed the steersman's ghost, and before long almost all the crew came to believe that the ship was haunted. Some even feared that the spirit was a bad omen, foretelling an imminent tragedy.

There were two men, however, who refused to believe in such nonsense. Their names were Robert Campbell and George Williams. They began to joke with the cabin boy about the ghost, and to alleviate the child's fear, Campbell placed his sharpened knife under his pillow, just in case the spirit appeared again the following night.

'Don't worry, lad,' he said. 'If I see it, I'll stab it and chuck it overboard!'

The Edinburgh police now believed they'd found their motive. Jean Moyatos had clearly overheard the conversation, and failing to completely understand what was being said, feared that the threats of stabbing and being thrown overboard were directed at him. Just hours after the misunderstanding had occurred, Moyatos stabbed Campbell and Williams before they had chance to do the same to him.

On being brought to trial before Scotland's High Court of Justiciary, Jean Moyatos was found to be insane, and was committed to a lunatic asylum.

Horrors of the Hulks

The transportation of convicts from the United Kingdom to His Majesty's colonies had taken place unofficially from as early as the 1600s. In 1717, Parliament passed the Transportation Act (otherwise known as 'An Act for the further preventing Robbery, Burglary, and other Felonies, and for the more effectual Transportation of Felons, and unlawful Exporters of Wool; and for declaring the Law upon some Points relating to Pirates'), establishing state-funded penal transportation to North America.

For a while this system ran quite smoothly, but in 1775, the American Revolutionary War broke out, disrupting the transportation of convicts, so hulk ships were introduced. These salvaged, often unseaworthy vessels served as temporary prisons until arrangements could be made to transport convicts to an appropriate penal colony, although in some cases sentences were carried out solely on board these vessels. They were moored offshore at various points across Britain, in close proximity to dockyards so the convicts could be sent to land and put to work, carrying out menial tasks for the benefit of the general public.

Upon arrival the prisoners were stripped, washed, given grey jackets and breeches to wear. They had irons clamped to their legs; and for every shilling they earned during their sentence, they were allowed to keep a penny. The remainder of the money was sent to the government, and the prisoners' sums were saved up and presented to them upon release.

By 1826, there were nine British hulks in regular use, housing a combined total of more than 3,000 convicted criminals; and a journalist for the *Kentish Chronicle* described how various recent 'improvements' had been made regarding the conditions on board. One amendment was the provision of separate vessels for criminal boys under the age of 14, and other vessels for the more 'depraved characters', who would have hitherto all been housed together in the same, overcrowded ship.

Food rations were meagre. Each man was permitted a daily serving of 1.25lb of bread, 2 pints of thick gruel and a small allowance of beer. Four days a week he was given 14oz of meat (which weighed considerably less when cooked), and on the other three days he had a quarter of a pound of cheese.

A terrible accident befell a hulk ship named the *Dolphin* on the morning of 16 October 1829. She was anchored in the Medway, and like most ships of her kind, was in a deplorable condition. In fact, she'd become so rundown and in need of repairs that she sprang a leak on her lower deck, and quickly began filling up. The leak went unnoticed by the officers on board, who only checked on the prisoners every half an hour, and rarely even ventured as far as the lower deck. The leak got worse and worse until eventually, in the early hours of the morning, the entire ship began to pitch. She became stuck in the mud and it was impossible for the crew to move her. Wondering what the matter could be, some of the crew began to investigate the cause of the pitching. They heard the cries of the prisoners coming from the lower deck, and one of the sailors went to quieten them down. It was only then the true extent of the calamity was discovered.

At first, Captain George Lloyd, the overseer of the ship, feared that more than a hundred men must have drowned in their cells. He ordered his crew to begin releasing the surviving prisoners at once. Six of the wards were duly unlocked, and in desperation the prisoners forced open a further two. Other convicts managed to escape through the ship's portholes, and swam to shore. As they'd been sleeping when the accident occurred, they reached land wearing nothing but their undergarments. They were rounded up by the military and marines, and forced to stand in their semi-naked condition for up to four hours, until order had been restored.

With everyone safely ashore, a party of rescuers returned to the vessel expecting to find hundreds of bodies, but the death toll was actually only three. Apart from one prisoner who was badly bruised, no one else suffered any serious injuries. The hulk was patched up and the convicts were eventually returned to their cells to continue their grim sentences.

In March 1856, a convict named Thomas Jones, who was imprisoned on board the *Stirling Castle* at Portsmouth, was accused of murdering the ship's surgeon, Charles William Hope.

The *Stirling Castle* was an invalid prison ship, to where criminals from other hulks were sent for treatment when they were seriously unwell. Jones was being treated by Mr Hope, who soon noticed some improvement in his patient's condition, and decided to transfer him from the lower deck, the home of the most grievously ill patients who were exempt from manual labour, to another part of the ship known as the 'class'. Here, the convalescents were given undemanding but regular jobs to perform until they were well enough to return to full-time labour.

Jones, however, resented this decision, preferring to stay on the lower deck, where he didn't have to lift a finger. He demanded for Hope to reconsider his diagnosis, but the surgeon refused. As the medic left the surgery, the prisoner followed him. When Jones was certain the coast was clear, he seized Hope with his left hand, and with his right, he slashed his victim's throat. The surgeon fell to the ground, where he bled to death.

Jones showed no remorse during his trial; in fact, he stated that the only thing he regretted was not being able to deliver the same fate to the entire crew of the hulk. Though Jones's lawyer argued that the prisoner was acting under some form of delusion, and was therefore not responsible for his actions, the jury returned an almost immediate verdict of guilty. The judge, having donned his black cap, sentenced the prisoner to death.

In February the following year, *The Sheffield Daily Telegraph* reported on a desperate escape attempt made by the prisoners on board an Australian hulk at Williamstown, Victoria.

The ringleader of the attempted breakout went by the name of Melville, though many suspected his real name was actually Thomas Smith. Either way, his accumulated sentences amounted to thirty-two years, but being quite mature of age, he wasn't expected to live to see the day of his release. So nefarious was this individual that he was assigned to the *President*, a specially designated hulk for the detention of only the most hardened criminals. Here, prisoners were locked inside strong, iron cells and chained to the solid timber of the ship. Escape was futile, but after a time, Melville succeeded in persuading his warders that he was a reformed man. He'd spent the past few months diligently transcribing passages from the Scriptures, and his efforts were finally rewarded when he was downgraded and transferred to the prison hulk *Success*, which accommodated the second highest category of prisoners.

Discipline here was slightly less harsh, and the inmates were put to hard labour instead of being kept in continual confinement.

One day, a chain gang of prisoners from the *Success* went to Williamstown to break stone; and at five o'clock in the afternoon it was time for them to return. A small boat, manned by four boatmen, had come to row the prisoners back to the hulk. The boat was attached to a launch by a long tow rope, and the prisoners were ordered to get into the launch fifty at a time. Melville was among the first batch of men in the launch, along with an officer named Jackson, who was charged with keeping an eye on the captives.

When the launch was about 200 yards from the shore, the prisoners, incited by Melville, began to heave on the tow rope in an attempt to close the gap between the launch and the rowing boat. One of the boatmen, Owen Owens, called for help, and Jackson tried to restore order, but he was seized by Melville and thrown overboard. He began swimming towards the rowboat, but the convicts got there first. The officer tried to pull himself into the little wooden

craft, but Melville grabbed him again and held him underwater. He eventually managed to free himself from the prisoner's grasp, but Owens wasn't so lucky. He too was thrown into the sea, along with his three colleagues, and according to the newspaper report, 'his brains were beaten out by one of the prisoners' who was still in possession of one of the stone-breaking hammers. Jackson and the other three seamen were later rescued, but it seemed that the captives were about to get away with their crime.

Safely aboard their hijacked rowing boat, the prisoners cut the tow rope and set sail, bound for freedom.

'*Adieu*, Victoria, at last!' cried Melville, blowing a triumphant kiss towards the hulk as his boat sailed away into the distance.

The hulk masters, however, weren't going to take the loss of one of their crew lightly. The water police were summoned and a number of officers gave chase, opening fire on the escaping convicts. One of the prisoners was killed and another gravely wounded, a bullet having passed through his neck. Eventually the police overtook the hijacked boat and arrested all on board.

Melville and nine of his confederates were tried for murder and sentenced to death at the scaffold, but according to a report in *The Morning Post*, their lives were spared at the eleventh hour, and they spent their remaining days under lock and key.

♪ The Skipper's Song ♪

Air – *Obvious*
Printed in *The Guernsey Star*, 27 May 1876

A death on the Ocean Wave
And a grave in the rolling deep,
For the Skipper whose owners save
On a foreign crew, dirt cheap!
I've French, Dutch, Turk, and Greek,
Swede, Fin, and Portugee –
And all the lingoes they speak
Are heathen Greek to me!
So a death on the Ocean Wave,
And a grave in the rolling deep,
When I'm knived or knocked on the head,
Some night, when no watch I keep.

For they all of 'em wear long knives,
And some have got pistols too,
And mine and my mates' dear lives
Aren't worth a tobaccy-screw!
They will take us unawares,
Like stuck pigs we shall die,
With no time to say our prayers,
And no chance to exchange 'Good-bye'.
For a death on the Ocean Wave,
And a grave in the rolling deep,
Is the skipper's whose owners save
On a foreign crew, dirt cheap!

Alone in a Haunted Hulk

It was 24 December 1888, and a hunter, in search of a juicy duck to take home for Christmas dinner, stumbled across an abandoned 200-ton hulk ship that had been left to rot upon the muddy bed of a lonely creek. This was his chance, he thought: he'd sneak on board and wait for an unsuspecting flock of ducks to appear.

In his little punt he propelled himself through the mud towards the crumbling old vessel that, even after years of solitude, still lay almost upright. He managed to navigate his boat across a little channel of water beside the starboard quarter, and was then able to clamber on board via the ship's rusty fore-chains.

It was clear that the ship would never be used again: the floor of the deck had crumbled away; her gear and rigging was all rotten; and scavengers had long since relieved her of anything of value.

'To me there is always a world of romance in a deserted ship,' the hunter told *The Leicester Chronicle & Leicestershire Mercury*. 'The places she has been to, the scenes she has witnessed, the possibilities of crime, of adventure – all these thoughts crowded upon me when I saw the old hulk lying deserted and forgotten.'

As tempting as it was to explore further, he heard a quack coming from below: the ducks had arrived! He knew this was his chance. He took aim and was about to pull his trigger when an enormous splash caused the flock of birds to depart in a flurry of feathers.

What could have caused the splash? The hunter hadn't dropped anything, and there was quite clearly nobody else in the vicinity. He surveyed the scene around him. All was still and quiet, and a chill breeze was bringing with it an early evening mist. The hunter knew it was time to be getting home before the daylight faded, but just then an extraordinary spectacle caught his eye: a punt on the river was gliding past, but there was nobody in her. The hunter was suddenly struck by a dreadful sense of realization: it was his boat. He must have forgotten to properly secure it when he clambered aboard the hulk. How on earth would he get home now?

Gripped with anxiety, and with dozens of desperate scenarios running through his mind, the hunter suddenly felt as though he wasn't alone. A mixture of strange noises began drifting over the boardless floor of the empty hull. It sounded as though someone – or something – was dragging a heavy weight towards him, and he could discern other noises, too. Was that a scream? Though he'd never been in the presence of a killer, thank goodness, the hunter supposed that the noises he could hear wouldn't have sounded out of place at the scene of a murder.

'I could hear a sound as of someone breathing slowly, stertorously,' he said; 'then a dull groan. And the cruel sodden blows fell, followed by a drip, drip, and heavy drop in the dank water below, from which the sickening smell rose, pungent, reeking, horrible.'

The terrified man huddled himself in a corner of the ship, his gun at the ready. The haunting sounds grew louder and louder, nearer and nearer, until the 'presence' seemed so close he could almost touch it. He lashed out with the barrel of his gun, but it passed through nothing but thin air.

Just then it felt as though something warm and wet like a drop of blood touched his forehead. He glanced up but saw only the dusky sky. Unwilling to remain on the vessel a moment longer, the hunter sprang to his feet, and taking his chances, leapt overboard, landing in the soft mud below. He made it to shore and dashed straight home, vowing never to return to that abandoned old hulk again.

Legends from the Sea

Almost every country across the world has its own legends and folktales, and the sea is no different. Every nationality of sailor can recount his own seafaring legend, and in the nineteenth century, seamen would amuse themselves by singing songs and sharing these timeless stories under the stars.

Sailors from the island of Sylt, in the North Sea, have an ageless legend that compares the sky to the roof of a gigantic house; the earth its foundations. Each night, when the sun disappears over the westerly edge of the roof, it is caught by the souls of recently departed virgin maidens. Perhaps out of wanton mischief, they proceed to tear up the sun, scattering the tiny pieces all around. Without the sun, the great house is plunged into darkness, so the souls of all the recently departed bachelors begin to gather up the sun-confetti. They spend the rest of the night climbing up and down an enormous ladder, sticking the little pieces on to the roof of the house, so there would at least be starlight after dark.

English sailors have their own legend about an enormous ship known as the *Mary Dunn*, of Dover, which once sailed in the English Channel. She was said to have had three decks and no bottom. So colossal was the vessel that when the wind blew, her boom – the long pole at the bottom of her sail – could touch the White Cliffs of Dover; when it blew in the opposite direction, it skirted the coast of Calais. Her deck was so long that the crew had to travel around on horseback, and her mast so tall that if a cabin boy dared to climb to the top, he'd return as a grey-haired old man.

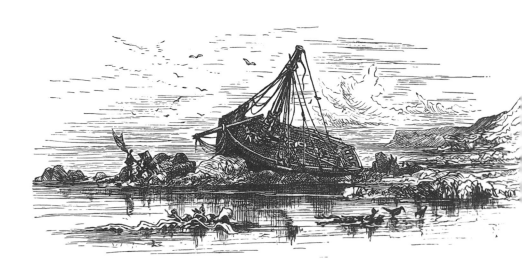

♪ *The Secret of the Sea* ♪

Longfellow
Printed in the *Nairnshire Telegraph*, 2 December 1868

Ah, what pleasant visions haunt me,
As I gaze upon the sea!
All the old romantic legends,
All my dreams, come back to me.

Sails of silk and ropes of sendal,
Such as gleam in ancient lore;
And the singing of the sailors
And the answers from the shore!

Most of all, the Spanish ballad
Haunts me oft, and tarries long,
Of the noble Count Arnaldos,
And the sailor's mystic song.

Like the long waves on a sea-beach,
Where the sand as silver shines,
With a soft monotonous cadence,
Flow its unrhymed lyric lines:–

Telling how the Count Arnaldos,
With his hawk upon his hand,
Saw a fair and stately galley,
Steering onward to the land:–

How he heard the ancient helmsman
Chant a song so wild and clear,
That the sailing sea-bird slowly
Poised upon the mast to hear.

Till his soul was full of longing,
And he cried with impulse strong –
'Helmsman, for the love of heaven,
Teach me, too, that wondrous song!'

'Wouldst thou,' so the helmsman answered,
'Learn the secrets of the sea?
Only those who brave its dangers
Comprehend its mystery.'

In each sail that skims the horizon,
In each landward-blowing breeze,
I behold that stately galley,
Hear those mournful melodies;

Till my soul is full of longing
For the secret of the sea,
And the heart of the great ocean
Sends a thrilling pulse through me.

The Fate of Seaside Fortune Tellers

In the nineteenth and early twentieth centuries, seaside towns were infested with fortune tellers who travelled to the coast for the summer months in the hope of earning a fortune by offering readings to unsuspecting visitors on the lookout for fun. Whilst some of these self-termed psychics brought comfort and entertainment, others, after having their palms crossed with copious amounts of silver, relished in telling dark tales of impending woe, which caused a deal of distress to sitters of a nervous disposition.

One day during the 1920s, a young woman on holiday in Blackpool went to visit 'Madame Dean' to have her fortune told. When she emerged from the tent she was visibly distressed and cried for days. She wouldn't eat, leave the house or sleep by herself. She eventually admitted to her mother that Madame Dean had told her she'd be dead within three months, and the young woman was so affected by her words that she broke off her engagement, unwilling to leave her fiancé a widower. After forecasting the deaths of two other people, the psychic, whose real name was Emily Holden, was arrested and fined £5.

By 1924, the public had become so sick and tired of being duped and upset by these seaside charlatans that local police forces had become overrun with complaints. In order to deal with the situation, detectives began employing family members to help them trap the phoney psychics. The officers felt that sitting for readings themselves would arouse suspicion, as it was generally women who consulted clairvoyants, so they sent their wives on top-secret undercover missions, often with remarkable results.

One of the most successful decoys was the wife of an officer from Sussex, who managed to secure a great number of convictions. Her name was Mrs Milton, and one day she was sent to trap a seaside palmist who confidently told her not to worry for she wouldn't remain a spinster much longer: a tall, dark, handsome stranger was waiting just around the corner … as was a police officer, who promptly arrested the palmist.

On another occasion, a police officer's wife named Mrs Dunham visited a male fortune teller at Cleethorpes. He was a shoemaker during the rest of the year, but in the summer he styled himself 'Professor Sargeant', and was quite a hit with the public. After charging her a shilling, the phrenologist removed Mrs Dunham's hat and proceeded to feel the bumps on her head before gazing intently at her palm.

'You're a woman in your fifties,' he told her. 'You're a sweet person but I sense you have a slight deceptive streak. You have remarkable powers of observation, so much so that if you'd been a man, you'd have made a great detective. Your husband trusts you implicitly, and I can see a happy future ahead.'

Mrs Dunham left the tent feeling as though Professor Sargeant had been remarkably accurate, until another policeman's wife, Mrs Wilkinson, went for a reading and came away with exactly the same message, word for word. The fortune teller was duly hauled before Grimsby County Police Court and fined 30 shillings plus costs, with the warning that if he continued plying his dubious trade, he'd receive a harsher punishment.

There was only one fortune teller who managed to escape conviction. She was of Hindu origin and traded under the name 'The Fascinating Smarina', and was so convincing that the detective's wife couldn't find fault. The psychic took hold of her sitter's hand and told her that many years ago her father had loved a dark Irish girl, but she'd died before they could marry. The woman had come from a wealthy family, and she'd left the sitter's father a great deal of money, which he'd used to set up a business in England.

At first the detective's wife thought this was nothing but a load of old nonsense, and was confident that she'd gathered enough evidence for her husband to make an arrest. She went straight to her father's home and delighted in telling him the lies she'd been told, only for her red-faced father to admit that it was all true. He'd never shared this secret with anyone, not even his wife and children. How 'The Fascinating Smarina' had come by this information, he couldn't explain, and neither could the baffled police authorities.

A Seaside Murder and a Continental Affair

It was seven o'clock in the evening on Monday, 22 September 1902, and a Parisian stockbroker named Lucien David was taking a stroll with his wife along the pleasant seafront at Étretat, France, overlooking the English Channel. They were taking in the bracing sea air when a well-known artist and painter named Jean Baptiste Syndon approached the couple and pulled a gun on Monsieur David. After exchanging a few violent words, the gunman squeezed the trigger and his victim fell dead to the ground, the bullet having passed right through the base of his neck.

Syndon fled from the scene of the crime, but an hour later he gave himself up to the gendarmerie at Bordeaux-Saint-Clair, a village 2 miles inland from

Étretat. When questioned, he simply declared that an overwhelming desire for vengeance was his motive for committing the murder.

The only witness to the incident was Madame David, formerly Miss Ehrenberg, but she claimed she didn't know of any reason why this attractive young man, who she'd certainly never set eyes on before in her entire life, would have wanted to kill her husband. She suggested Monsieur Syndon must have been suffering from some strange delusion or homicidal mania, for she could think of no other explanation.

The gendarmes, however, weren't so convinced, and a thorough inquiry was launched. It wasn't long before details of the murder became public knowledge, and the exclusive seaside resort was thrown into a state of commotion and intrigue. Why on earth would a talented painter like Monsieur Syndon, a former student of the great Léon Bonnat, wish to kill such an eminent businessman? Monsieur David was well respected in the financial circles of Paris and London, and as far as anyone knew, had no quarrel with anyone.

It soon became evident that Syndon had been on familiar terms with the David family for quite some time, despite Madame David's claim to the contrary. Her brother, Monsieur Ehrenberg, was a ship owner, who some months earlier had arranged for Syndon to embark on a round-the-world cruise. Syndon was suffering from ill health, and Monsieur David suggested that the artist should spend some time in San Francisco, where he might find the climate to his liking. As soon as he began to feel better, he returned to France, and was commissioned by the stockbroker to paint a portrait of his wife. He was even invited to stay with the family while he worked on his masterpiece.

The Davids left Paris for Étretat on Saturday, 20 September, and Syndon arrived in town two days later, seemingly in search of his victim. He proceeded to Villa Louise, the seaside summer home of Madame and Monsieur David and their four children. A servant answered the door, and Syndon enquired after Madame David. He was told that she'd gone out for an evening walk with her husband, so the would-be killer went in search of the couple, eventually finding them by the seafront.

A warrant was issued, and the artist's home and studio in Paris were searched from top to bottom. Just when it seemed as though there was nothing of interest to be found, the police discovered a stash of potentially incriminating letters. One of the senders was none other than Monsieur David. He'd written to Syndon expressing his displeasure at the amount of time the artist was spending with his 15-year-old daughter, Marcelle, who was taking art lessons from him. He ended the communication by telling Syndon he was no longer welcome in his house.

The gendarmes had a motive at last. They put it to the accused that he'd been so fiercely denounced by his former friend that he lost control of himself, drawing a revolver and shooting David dead without realizing what he was doing. Syndon hesitated before simply stating that he had nothing more to say on the matter.

Fortunately for the prosecution, Syndon's sister, a dressmaker from Paris, was willing to give evidence. She claimed it wasn't true about her brother forming a relationship with Mademoiselle David, but he had used the art lessons as an excuse to get close to the girl's mother, Madame David. An intrigue had been going on for several years, but overwhelmed with guilt, the artist tried many times to end the liaison; he even travelled abroad in the hope that absence would cure him of his lust, but he returned to France more enamoured than ever. He used the pretext of giving regular drawing lessons to the couple's daughter in order to get close to the mistress of the house, who he'd come to realize he was unable to live without.

Syndon's increasing attachment to the family was becoming a source of irritation for the head of the household who, by now, was keen to see the back of the young, talented and handsome painter who'd overstayed his welcome.

Whenever she had the opportunity to sneak away, Madame David used to visit her lover at his mother's flat on Boulevard Exelmans, Paris, where he lived. Neighbours confirmed that an elegantly dressed woman, apparently a few years older than Syndon, was a regular visitor to the flat, though she always wore a veil so she wouldn't be recognized. Her visits became so incessant that Madame Syndon, who disapproved of her son's affair, eventually moved out. Though his family did everything they could to dissuade the young man from carrying on with his imperious mistress, the artist refused to listen. He was so besotted that he started carrying around a photograph of Madame David, which was found in his possession when he was arrested.

A sculptor named Monsieur Chartrain, who worked in a studio adjoining Syndon's on the Avenue de Versailles, claimed to have seen a smart and extremely angry sounding man on his neighbour's doorstep on 18 September, just days before the murder took place; and the next time Chartrain saw Syndon, he was carrying a revolver, which the artist claimed he'd sourced in order to protect himself against muggers. He was later spotted practising with it in the garden of the studio.

The gendarmes concluded that the smartly dressed man was Monsieur David, who, suspecting something was going on with Syndon and Marcelle, went to confront the man face to face. A fierce argument ensued, and when David returned home, he instructed his family to pack their bags for Étretat. The infuriated artist, determined to resolve matters once and for all, followed by train a couple of days later, his revolver safely stowed in his pocket.

When the case went to court, the accused repeatedly refused to explain his actions, citing the honour of Madame David as the reason for his silence. The deceased's widow was too ill to attend the trail, which lasted two days; and in November 1902, Jean Baptiste Syndon was found guilty of wilful homicide, and sentenced to ten years' penal servitude. He never saw Madam David again.

Villa Louise still stands in Étretat. It was converted into a luxury boutique guesthouse during the twentieth century and renamed the Hotel Ambassadeur, affording guests the perfect opportunity to explore the beautiful coastline of Étretat, where its former owner met such an untimely end more than a century ago.

♪ The Lady Rosalie ♪

G. Weatherly
Printed in *Family Magazine*, 1881

The wind crept softly over the sea,
With stealthy tread, so treacherously,
And its steps gleamed white
In the shimmering light
Of the silver moon;
And the sea was crooning a lullaby
Of a maiden bright,
Fair to the sight
As a sunny noon:
'*O sweetest of sweet maidens she!*
Sweet is the Lady Rosalie!

'Each night she comes and stands by me,
And tells me all her misery,
With questioning eyes,
And 'plaining cries
Like caged bird's song:
"O sea, sea, sea! O cruel sea!
Bring him to me!
Why tarries he
So long, so long?"
O saddest of sad maidens she!
Sad is the Lady Rosalie!

'And now she sleeps upon the strand,
Her fair head pillowed on the sand,
And in her ear
I whisper clear:
"Your lover's true!
From other clime and other land,
Across the track
I bring him back
To love and you!"

O gladdest of glad maidens she!
Glad is the Lady Rosalie!'

The wind strode fiercely over the sea,
With mighty tread, so cruelly!
And, tempest-tossed,
A ship was lost
Beneath the wave.
Then he laughed aloud in savage glee:
'O pitying sea,
Where now is he
Whom you would save?
Saddest of maidens will she be!
Your own fair Lady Rosalie!'

The morn is bright, and by the sea
One walks with Lady Rosalie;
And in her eyes
The love-light lies,
And glad her song:
'O kindly sea, so dear to me,
Since you have brought
Him whom I sought
So long, so long!
O gladdest of glad maidens she!
The happy Lady Rosalie!'

The Vanishing Cornish Girl

In the springtime of 1922, Cornwall's hottest topic of discussion was a seaside mystery that had everyone baffled. An attractive young woman named Mollie Ombler, who was living on Harbour Crescent, Newquay, with her widowed mother, had vanished into the night on Thursday, 1 June without a trace, and no one could offer any kind of explanation as to why or where she'd gone. The police were perplexed, and after combing Cornwall without success, the search was widened to cover three counties.

A description of Miss Ombler was circulated in the press. She was described as having rosy cheeks, brown eyes and black hair, and stood about 5ft 4in tall. She was 27 years old, had a full, healthy figure, and was last seen wearing a biscuit-coloured dress decorated with blue roses, a large opal brooch, white silk stockings and black satin slippers.

Her mother, Mrs Lydia Pearce, had last seen Mollie at about ten o'clock on the night she vanished. The young woman had gone into her mother's bedroom to complain about the heat, and said she was going to go downstairs to get a glass of water. Her mother thought nothing more about it, and went back to sleep.

The following morning, a housemaid went into Miss Ombler's bedroom with her usual cup of tea, but there was no sign of the expected occupant. It was clear her bed hadn't been slept in, and her nightclothes were still neatly folded on the pillow. The maid alerted Mrs Pearce at once, who searched the property, looking for clues. She deduced that her daughter must have left the house without a hat and shoes, for no items of clothing were missing except for her slippers and the outfit she was last seen wearing. What was more, she hadn't taken her pursebag, so Mrs Pearce refused to believe her daughter had run away. It didn't appear she'd been abducted either: the family had a pet dog who'd certainly have barked if anyone had approached the house, but he'd remained silent all night.

Mollie, the only daughter from a previous marriage, was a vivacious young woman without any known cares or worries, and as far as anyone knew, she didn't have any love interests. She was a talented pianist with a promising future ahead; and the only change in her behaviour was that she'd recently started complaining about having headaches and bouts of insomnia.

Mrs Pearce offered £100 in reward money for anyone with information that would lead to her daughter being found alive, and £20 if she was found dead. As soon as news of this generous recompense began to spread, hundreds of people got to work, scouring miles and miles of coastland in the hope of locating some kind of clue, but nothing was found. This led investigators to assume that Miss Ombler almost certainly hadn't been drowned at sea.

Police thus turned their attention inland, and a new lead was discovered. On 24 May, Mollie travelled by train from Paddington, where she'd been working as a lady's companion, to Newquay, to spend a few weeks' holiday with her mother. There were two other people in her compartment: a man and a young girl. During the latter part of the journey, after the other two passengers had left, a witness overheard Mollie ask the train guard if she could be locked alone in her carriage, as she was feeling a little nervous. He duly obliged. When the train pulled into the next station, a man was seen approaching the window of her compartment, and was heard to say to her: 'Anyway, I shall see you at Newquay.'

Though the police had no idea who this man could have been, the young girl who was travelling with Mollie was traced and questioned. She'd alighted at Teignmouth, before the train had reached Newquay, and remembered Miss Ombler because she'd been kind enough to offer the young girl assistance when she started feeling travelsick. However, she insisted that they were the only two passengers in the carriage for the entirety of the journey. At no time was a man travelling with them, and the girl certainly didn't see anyone speak to her companion.

It wasn't long before police started receiving dozens of reported sightings of Mollie from all over the country, and on 12 June the mystery of the beautiful young woman's whereabouts was finally solved. Three local fishermen spotted something bobbing up and down in the water by Old Dane Rock and went to investigate. Though it was completely covered in seaweed, it was clearly the body of a young woman matching Mollie's description. They pulled it from the ocean and wrapped it in a sail before bringing it ashore and alerting the police.

The body was battered and bruised beyond recognition. Her identity was only confirmed by the biscuit-coloured dress and opal brooch she was still wearing; her stockings and slippers had gone.

Mollie's body was taken to the mortuary, where investigators hoped to find some answers, but instead they were faced with even more questions. The girl's left arm was thrown across her face, in a protective position, and rigor mortis had caused it to become so firmly fixed that straightening it was an impossible task. This was something the police couldn't explain. If Mollie had slipped and fallen from the cliff, she would have landed either in the sea or on the rocks, depending on the tide. Either way, her arm certainly wouldn't have remained at that angle: if she'd landed in the water, the waves would have swept it from her face, and if she'd landed on the beach, the impact of the rocks would have forced her arm away from her head.

The post-mortem examination revealed that Mollie had been alive for at least five hours after she'd eaten her last meal. Mollie and her mother had dined at eight o'clock on 1 June, leading investigators to conclude that the young woman probably died at about one o'clock in the morning of 2 June. This was most baffling, for Mrs Pearce insisted that her daughter was mortally afraid of two things: the dark and thunder. It was a hot, dark and stormy night when she vanished, so what could have possessed her to leave the house at that time and in that weather?

The place where her body was found was close to the Atlantic Hotel, at Newquay Bay, where the cliffs were 1,000ft high. Curiously, the body of another young woman had been pulled from the exact same spot a decade earlier. Her name was Mrs Nowill, and like Mollie, the circumstances surrounding her disappearance were most peculiar indeed. Then, in 1921, a local nurse vanished from Newquay and was presumed dead. By some bizarre coincidence she was discovered, alive and well, by the same three fishermen who found Mollie's body. The nurse had slipped from a cliff and had landed on a narrow ledge, where she'd remained for seventy-two hours before being spotted and rescued.

An inquest was held on 13 June, and an open verdict was returned. All the evidence pointed to Mollie being a bright and happy girl, and as the police had failed to produce any murder suspects, it was assumed that she must have wandered out on to the cliffs during a bout of temporary lunacy, and stumbling about in the darkness, lost her footing. Whatever happened that night, the grave question of how exactly Mollie Ombler met her end remains unanswered to this day.

Mrs Nowill and the Cliffside Felo-De-Se

It was an unseasonably warm November in 1912 when Sidney Nowill, a successful merchant of Sandygate House, Sheffield, stood at the smoky railway station and waved his wife and mother-in-law goodbye. They were heading to Newquay for a few days, and were looking forward to a little break; but unbeknown to Mr Nowill, his wife had other things planned than just pleasant walks on the promenade.

Mrs Nowill was a wealthy and attractive 35-year-old. About two years earlier she and her husband had travelled to Egypt. During the long voyage they befriended a solicitor named James Arthur Delay, and they'd stayed in touch ever since. The trio had met socially after returning to England, but Mr Nowill had no idea just how friendly his wife and the 46-year-old solicitor had become; the pair grew so close, in fact, that Mr Delay added a codicil to his Last Will and Testament declaring that upon his death the married lady should receive £30,000 – roughly half the value of his entire personal estate.

It just so happened that Mr Delay was staying in Newquay when Mrs Nowill and her mother arrived. Not wanting to waste this opportune 'coincidence', the clandestine lovers made the most of their brief time together. They checked into the Atlantic Hotel and were last spotted by the manageress at 4.45 on the afternoon of Saturday, 23 November. Soon afterwards, Mrs Nowill had vanished.

A search party was formed later that evening, and vast stretches of coastland were combed. As the hours ticked by, and no sign of the missing woman materialized, Mr Delay became hysterical. He rounded on the coastguard, threatening to kill him if he didn't do something, and fast. The officer tried to assure him that he was doing everything in his power to find Mrs Nowill, but this wasn't enough for the solicitor, and out of sheer desperation he attempted to throw himself off a cliff. The coastguard tried to stop him, and a frantic clifftop struggle ensued. After several critical moments, Mr Delay was restrained and escorted back to his hotel room, utterly exhausted.

The following day, the police appealed for information and a witness came forward, claiming to have seen a couple matching the descriptions of Mr Delay and Mrs Nowill shortly before the lady vanished. They were walking together by the shore, and though they were out of earshot, they appeared to have been embroiled in a bitter altercation. On several occasions, the gentleman, after walking a few yards, tried to take hold of the lady's hand, but she repeatedly pushed him away.

There was still no sign of the missing woman two days later, and the tragedy intensified when Mr Delay's body was found hanging in his hotel room. An inquest was held on 27 November, when the jury returned a verdict of felo de se; in other words, suicide.

In the first week of December, local newspapers announced that the recent Newquay sensation had reached a dramatic conclusion: Mrs Nowill's body had been discovered. The sea gave up its dead on 2 December; her remains were found among the rocks and breakers, just below the cliff upon which the Atlantic Hotel stood. Her body was taken home to Sheffield, where her funeral took place, her widower having never learned the true circumstances surrounding his wife's untimely demise.

Though an exact date of death was unclear, Mr Nowill persuaded the coroner to certify his late wife's death as 23 November, two days before Mr Delay's. This meant that as the late solicitor outlived his intended beneficiary, Mrs Nowill's estate was not legally entitled to inherit his generous bequest of £30,000. Whilst the testator explained in his will that the sum was intended as 'a slight token of the high admiration and esteem' he held for her, and the gratitude he felt for the friendship she'd shown him over the past few years, Mr Nowill refused point blank to accept the legacy. Mr Delay's fortune was subsequently inherited by his widow, Mrs Mary Delay. This was another mystery entirely, for none of Mr Delay's family or friends had any idea he was married!

♪ Good-bye ♪

G.W.
Printed in *Family Magazine*, 1875

The sun in the sky above shines bright,
Its glancing rays of golden light
Gleam all around;
And the dancing sunbeams softly fleck,
With many a shadowy line, the deck
Of an Outward Bound.

A sailor and his wife stand there,
Her face all sad with grief and care
And troublous fears;
Their little child, with glance up-bent,
Looks on in curious wonderment
To see her tears.

'Good-bye! good-bye!' the sailor cries;
'Let not the tear-drops dew thine eyes,
My own sweet wife;
One last fond kiss before we part,
Press close to mine thy beating heart,
And still its strife.

'My comfort, darling, is to know
It is not death that parts me so
From thy sweet face;
A few months hence, and o'er the sea
The waves will bring me back to thee,
To rest and peace.'

Alas, brave heart! but three days more,
And the waves *had* brought thee back to shore,
But not in life!
And the sun went down in radiance wild
On the faces of thine orphaned child
And weeping wife.

The Life-Saving Seaside Donkeys

Donkey rides have been a popular seaside attraction since Victorian times, and donkey owners up and down the country found that a decent wage could be earned by offering young children a jaunt along the sandy beaches. Whilst most youngsters derived nothing but pleasure from the experience, there was one child who owed his life to this quaint little seaside tradition.

On the night of 6 April 1937, Great Ormond Street Hospital issued a wireless appeal to any donkey owners who could spare some milk to feed a dying baby boy. The little orphan wasn't capable of digesting cows' milk, and as doctors believed that asses' milk was similar in composition to human milk, they felt that the child stood a decent chance of survival if a supplier was found. They didn't hold out much hope, however, for it wasn't the season for foals, and it was therefore unlikely that any jennies were lactating.

A donkey owner from Bridlington heard the appeal. It just so happened that one of his seaside jennies had recently given birth to a foal out of season. The young creature was immediately put on a diet of cows' milk and reared by hand, enabling the owner, Mr Carvill, to send the jenny's milk to the capital. The first pint and a half was put on the first train to London, and Mr Carvill promised a fresh supply every day for as long as the hospital needed it.

Another seaside donkey owner, Mr George Jones, from Rhyl, was in the same position. His pet's name was Dolly, and she too had given birth, so Mr Jones agreed to send a daily pint of milk until the child got better.

Sure enough, the boy's condition began to improve, and he was declared fit and healthy by September the following year. A photograph of Dolly was sent to him as a little memento, so he'd always remember the seaside donkey that helped to save his life.

Musicians of the Sands

Seaside towns were popular holiday destinations for Victorian families, particularly ones who lived in the inner cities, which were full of smog, noise and disease. Yearning for a change of scene and some fresh salty air, people would flock in their thousands to sample the summer delights of coastal resorts.

Eager to take full advantage of these seasonal tourists, troupes of musicians would also journey to the coast during the summer. They'd set up their instruments by the beach and serenade passers-by, in the hope that a copper or two might be flung in their direction. In some resorts, this turned out to be a lucrative business indeed. One such musician, according to the 8 September 1893 edition of *The Lancashire Daily Post*, was a talented singer and pianist, and he earned £8 a week – that would be the equivalent of about £790 today.

'He generally gets good audiences, does not work too hard, and is careful with his resources,' said the paper's reporter. 'He looks on these "tours" as a profitable way of utilizing summer months, which in London would be anything but productive.'

As *The Cornishman* explained, on 24 August 1899, seaside musicians would 'generally begin work at eleven in the morning and play till one, begin again at three and play till five.' Some bands went out again after dinner and performed two or three evening shows.

ON THE BEACH

Though many visitors enjoyed these musical treats, to others, they were nothing but an audible nuisance.

'[The seaside's] musical surroundings are awful, ghastly, exasperating, intolerable, and of them there is no end,' said a correspondent of *The Morning Post*, printed on 1 October 1888. 'The instruments of torture are so scientifically posted that do what you will, you cannot get clear of them, as you rush in terror from one, you fall in agony into the arms of another.'

He went on to suggest that the musicians might make even more money if they changed their tactics by holding up placards reading: 'Give me a penny and I *won't* play'.

Further grievances were voiced in Yorkshire during the summer of 1894, when a troupe of ragtag musicians set themselves up on a previously tranquil stretch of beach. Irate correspondents of *The Dundee Evening Telegraph* complained of 'a hurdy-gurdy boy dancing and singing in Italian (it is supposed); a hurdy-gurdy girl with a monkey; four men with a piano, one of whom sang; an old organ, accompanied by a tall girl, dressed as a boy, who danced a Highland reel; and a trombone.'

The paper declared that all the instruments were extremely old and of poor quality, yet visitors were cheerfully expected to hand over their coins in return for this exclusive entertainment. It wasn't reported whether or not many Yorkshire folk, supposedly renowned for keeping their hands in their pockets, deigned to part with their hard-earned money.

♪ To a Sea-Shell ♪

J.W.M.

Printed in *Family Magazine*, 1885

O sea-shell, singing, as if in thy soul,
In a melodious low-voiced monotone,
Of sounding shores where foam-bright breakers roll,
Of sunlit seas where but wave-songs are known!
Thy crimson-wreathed ear, in days long flown,
Drank deep the wondrous music of the sea;
And now thy heart, with mingled mirth and moan,
Still sighing swells with ocean's melody.
A shell upon life's morning shore like thee,
The sad soul, severed from its natal bays,
Yet holds high treasured in dear memory
The glorious cadence of love's early lays,
And pleased in sorrow, listens to the low
Heart-holden symphonies of long ago.

The Great Sandcastle Dispute of 1900

Visitors to Rhyl during the summer of 1900 would have found some of its residents up in arms. Earlier that August, Bovril, the meat extract manufacturing company, organized a children's sandcastle building competition on the beach. They'd offered a substantial prize to the child who could build the most impressive sandcastle that bore the name of their product. So successful and well attended was the event that a local wine and spirit merchant, John Ellis, decided to host his own competition a few days later. Children of all ages were eligible to enter, providing they followed one rule: they had to incorporate the name of a well-known brand of whisky on the front of their castles. Some creative and attractive designs were made, and it seemed as though everyone had an enjoyable day.

That was until the following Sunday, when an indignation meeting was held by some of the area's most prominent temperance advocates, outraged that children were being encouraged to advertise alcohol.

'Innocent children were being made the medium for advertising one of the greatest curses of the country,' Reverend Cooper told *The Grantham Journal* on 1 September that year.

A most strongly worded letter was sent to Rhyl Council insisting that any future advertising competitions should be banned. This request, however, was dismissed at the next council meeting, angering the members of the Temperance Movement even more. In response, the party decided to host their own sandcastle competition, offering bigger and better prizes to the child who could build the best castle that denounced drink in the strictest possible terms.

To show he bore no ill feelings towards the Temperance Movement, Mr Ellis promised to reward the winner of this competition with a surprise gift, though what exactly the wine and spirit merchant offered as a prize wasn't disclosed by the papers.

The Lunatic in the Lighthouse

In August 1905, reports came flooding in from America concerning a lighthouse keeper named Mr Hulse, who worked at the Stratford Shoals Lighthouse in the middle of Long Island Sound, off the coast of New York City. According to a series of contemporary newspaper reports, he'd suffered a 'terrible week', for not only did he have to spend seven nights keeping the beacon light burning singlehandedly, he also had to prevent himself from being slain by his fellow lighthouse keeper, Mr Costler, who'd suddenly and inexplicably gone mad. For a whole week, Mr Hulse lived in constant danger of being murdered, and with no means of leaving Stratford Shoals until a boatman came to collect them – the lighthouse being situated on a small rock in the middle of the ocean – he didn't even dare sleep, not even for a moment.

It wasn't known exactly what triggered Mr Costler's madness, but one day while at work he began to imagine that he was the Archangel Gabriel, and that Mr Hulse was a dragon that couldn't be allowed to live any longer. Failing to fell the beast with a woodman's axe, he spent seven days and nights attempting to end his colleague's life with a selection of other weapons, including knives, sledgehammers and razor blades.

Mr Hulse fought valiantly to defend himself, and every now and again he succeeded in knocking Mr Costler unconscious, buying himself a few brief moments in which to dash to the lamp and keep the light burning. By the end of the week, when the relief party arrived, Mr Hulse was utterly exhausted. He was taken ashore in an almost insensible condition, and it was several days before he was able to relay an articulate account of his terrifying escapades.

Senior officials in the naval industry praised Mr Hulse for his selflessness. Though his own life had been in peril, he diligently kept the lighthouse running, thus preventing passing ships from being wrecked.

♪ Christopher Columbus ♪

George Weatherly
Printed in *Family Magazine*, 1887

Bold, resolute, and strong – a man, forsooth,
Of infinite resource to carry out
Whate'er his hand and brain had set about –
He lived among men ignorant, uncouth,
Yet kept the golden vision of his youth,
And toiled for bread, when skies were overcast,
Map-making, copying writings, till at last,
His master-purpose ripe, he proved its truth.

Then the astonished world, in strange amaze,
Heard whispers of the vast new continent,
Yet grudged the finder his due meed of praise!
Not so with us: we thank with glad intent
The bold discoverer who paved the way
For *two* great English-speaking lands to-day!

The Benefits of Sea Bathing

Sea bathing became a fashionable pastime in the eighteenth century when a couple of noted physicians, namely William Buchan and Dr Charles Russel, published books on the subject. Both men claimed that the natural minerals found in seawater could help to cure a variety of diseases and physical complaints, both internally and externally. This soon became a topic of research for family physicians, who began drawing their own conclusions and issuing their own pieces of advice to patients.

Before the 1700s had drawn to a close, a special sea-bathing establishment was opened in Margate, and by 1830, a similar institution began operating in the Yorkshire seaside town of Scarborough. This institution, known as the

Royal Northern Sea-Bathing Infirmary, was reserved for the use of the poor and destitute in desperate need of aid. As stated in the *Yorkshire Gazette* on 27 June 1840, it was a place where, under the supervision of a matron, 'the poor have the privilege of bathing, but nothing more'. Paupers who had to travel to the infirmary were reimbursed at the rate of twopence a mile for their travel expenses, and upon arrival they were offered warm seawater baths, along with tonics and medicines, gratuitously.

By the middle of the century, there was a public demand for such sea-bathing infirmaries to be opened in other seaside resorts so that the salubrious effects of the seaside could help to cure many more paupers across Britain.

It was generally accepted by nineteenth-century doctors that sea baths would treat invalids with any kind of impaired functional power. It was a known fact that, along with other beneficial ions and minerals, seawater contained traces of iodine, an essential element that was required for healthy growth and development.

According to a medical expert writing for *The Leeds Intelligencer*, sea bathing was an effective cure for diseased or injured limbs. He explained, on 30 May 1840, that saline water could alleviate pains and swellings of the joints. The ocean had also been observed to reduce inflammation of the eyes and glands; and regular dips would help to restore a person's general health and vigour. The correspondent even claimed that bathers who were 'seemingly at the brink of death' would emerge from the water feeling better than ever.

Medical opinion was that children, particularly incontinent and anaemic ones, and girls who suffered from chlorosis, would benefit from sea bathing. Doctors regularly advised young women who suffered from 'hysteria' that a dip in the sea would alleviate their symptoms, and patients with other forms of nervous disposition were also said to gain from this wholesome therapy. Furthermore, people suffering from colds and respiratory conditions often found relief at the seaside, as salt was known to be an effective decongestant.

Sea bathing, however, wasn't suitable for everyone. According to the *British Medical Journal*, an extract from which was printed in the *Northern Evening Mail* on 30 June 1883, people suffering from 'cerebral congestion', any kind of 'organic diseases of the heart', 'aneurism' or those who didn't possess 'the ability safely to encounter a comparatively severe shock' ought to avoid taking a dip. The journal also forbade women from entering the sea during 'certain periods in which the female constitution is not prepared for the application of powerful remedies'. Similarly, it was considered harmful to take babies and children under the age of two for a paddle, whilst the elderly were deemed far too frail to stand the shock of cold water.

In 1893, bathers were warned against getting their ears wet in the sea, for if the eardrum came into contact with too much saltwater, it was feared that earache or permanent deafness would follow. Numerous cases of brain inflammation had been attributed to seawater entering through the ear and travelling up into the cranium. Some bathers therefore chose to plug their ears with cotton wool before entering the ocean.

City dwellers diagnosed with fatigue due to the effects of overwork were generally advised to spend a season relaxing by the seaside. However, they were instructed not to even think of entering the sea until their bodies had become sufficiently invigorated by leisurely exercise in the fresh, open air. As soon as they'd developed a 'healthful glow', they were considered fit to enter the ocean.

A family doctor writing in *The Lancashire Gazette* on 23 August 1879 suggested that a bath of fresh seawater should be heated to a temperature of 90º Fahrenheit and the fatigued worker should bathe in it for ten minutes before getting out and rubbing him- or herself down with a rough towel. This should be repeated every forenoon for seven days consecutively, and by the end of the week, a person suffering from the ill effects of overwork should start to feel refreshed. If these daily ablutions were continued throughout the second week, using cold seawater instead of warm, then by the third week the patient would be ready to reap the benefits of bathing in the open sea.

Medical experts confirmed the best time for entering the ocean to be two hours after breakfast, on a warm and sunny day. It was just as dangerous to bathe on an empty stomach as it was a full one, so if the bather fancied a pre-breakfast dip, they were counselled to have a cup of coffee and a few biscuits before venturing forth.

It was better for bathers to plunge straight into the sea so that every part of their body was affected at the same time. By entering it gradually, their blood rushed straight to their head, causing congestion.

'Undress as quickly as possible and enter the water boldly, taking care to wet the top of the head, even if, in deference to luxurious tresses, a regular "dunk" is not effected,' advised a specialist writing in the *Coventry Herald* on 18 August 1893. They continued:

Take a succession of brisk dips, immersing the body quite up to the chin, and then retire to the [bathing] machine, having spent under five minutes in the water. A good rub down with rough bath towels and a speedy toilette complete the bathe for the time being, and immediately afterwards a sharp walk should be taken along the cliffs or beach, to restore the circulation, and the delightful feeling of exhilaration which inevitably follows will be sufficient evidence of the benefit of the bath.

The contributor went on to say that the length of time in the water could be gradually increased to half an hour, and if any sign of a chill was noticed, a nip of neat brandy should be taken while dressing.

Though bathers often found the coldness of the sea a little overwhelming at first, they were assured by the *Brighton Gazette* that this soon gave way to 'a desire for muscular exertion, and a feeling of lightness and strength'. Then, upon leaving the sea, the bather experienced 'a delightful glow on the surface of the body'. Their mind subsequently became 'excited with pleasurable emotions', whilst their heart rate and appetite increased, digestion improved and their general health was enriched.

Despite all these wondrous claims, concerns were raised in the summer of 1876 following several reported cases of bathers, unable to swim, drowning in the ocean. For the safety of invalids seeking solace in saltwater, *The Edinburgh Evening News* printed the following guidelines:

(1) Avoid beating upon the surface of the water but thrust the arms *completely below the water* as well as every other part of the body, except the head.
(2) Throw the head back as far as possible, turning the face right up to the sky.
(3) Except when shouting for help, keep the mouth closed, breathing rather through the nostrils.
(4) To balance the body the arms should be extended a little, and the hands may be moved in a 'paddling' manner, but always beneath the water.

Attention to these simple rules will keep anyone securely floating at the surface of the sea, however deep, with the head safely above, as if upon the softest of down and couches, for a very long time, in almost every case amply sufficient for an easy rescue.

According to the article, the human body was thought to be one-tenth lighter than saltwater. It thereby followed that if nine-tenths of the body were kept below the surface, the remaining fraction – the head and shoulders – would float; in other words, if everything but the head was always submerged, it was impossible to drown.

Electrolysed Seawater

In 1894, newspapers from around the world were awash with encouraging stories concerning a new development in sanitation. The previous year, a French researcher named Monsieur Hermite had discovered a new way of cleansing streets, sewers and other public places using electrolysed seawater. He'd discovered that by subjecting ordinary seawater to the action of electricity, the water became a powerful disinfectant, and he began large-scale trials at Le Havre on the coast of France.

The apparatus he used was similar to a container filled with platinum electrodes, which conveyed the electrical current, of around 100 volts, to the water as it passed through. Hermite connected his apparatus to a network of pipes, which were laid throughout the St François quarter of the city, which was at the time home to about 12,000 people. It was one of the poorest regions of Le Havre, where sanitation was virtually non-existent and infectious diseases plagued the streets. As soon as the electrolysed water was passed through the pipes and sprinkled on to the roadways, a marvellous change was said to have occurred. The putrid odour that once filled the alleyways was diminished, and the trial seemed so promising that the district's architect arranged for two of the most unwholesome dwellings to be fitted with their own domestic flushing systems. One of the properties was at 24 Rue Jean de la Fontaine and the other at 35 Rue d'Edreville, both within walking distance of the sea. Hermite fitted a large tank, connected to the electrolysed water mains, at the top of each of these six-storey buildings. This was used to flush the closets and sinks on each floor of the properties. The wastewater ran through the pipes into the gutters outside, before ending up in the sewer.

It was reported by *The Standard* on 7 May 1894 that a doctor had conducted a series of scientific tests to determine the effectiveness of Hermite's new system. He concluded that whilst there had been 'a remarkable reduction in the number of living microbes', the seawater disinfectant wasn't powerful enough to properly protect the public against the most resilient germs and diseases. Without any funding available to him, Hermite was forced to abandon his project.

♪ Ere the Night ♪

Isabella Banks

Printed in *Family Magazine*, 1875

I look out across the waters
To the gold and crimson west,
Where the regal sun is drawing
Evening's veil before his breast;
Ere, with kindly care for mortals
Who are weary and o'erworn,
He permits night's dusky portals
To close o'er him until morn;
And I gaze upon his glory
Till I feel no more forlorn.

I had been o'ertried and driven
Ere I brought my boat to shore,
For the wind had been untoward,
And the current mocked my oar;
But the baffling breeze tore past me,
Cheering zephyrs glassed the tide,
And ere evening's shades o'ercast me
I have touched the hither side,
And in yonder sunset glory
I see hope re-typified.

The Beach of a Million Stars

At daybreak on 29 December 1927, residents at Deal, the coastal town near Dover, were treated to a wondrous sight: the entire length of the beach, stretching 7 miles from Sandwich Bay to Kingsdown, was covered in a glistening display of frozen starfish. There were millions of them; they'd been washed up by the tide along with innumerable lobsters and other kinds of shellfish. In some places the starfish lay so thick that the sand on the beach was invisible.

This remarkable phenomenon was caused by a dreadful gale that had besieged the English Channel for the past four days. The powerful gusts of wind had disturbed the seabed, devastating the starfishes' breeding ground; and as each wave cast the creatures on to land, the winter frost caused them to freeze.

Coral Houses

In the West Indies during the 1880s it was found that common white coral made an excellent material for building houses. This led the local authorities in that part of the world, and in other tropical regions where coral was plentiful, to propose that the material ought to be put to good use in the construction industry. Builders in Bermuda duly began erecting houses using coral that had been washed up on the beach. The material was found to be exceptionally durable, and besides being a glorious shade of white, it was permeable by air, so the rooms inside were cool, airy and light.

A type of heavy, non-porous coral known as 'brain-stone', so called because of its brain-like appearance, was used for doorsteps, roads and pathways. It was also used to build sea walls with, owing to its exceptional durability against the destructive power of the waves.

One of the most notable coral structures still standing today is Coral Castle in Leisure City, Florida. It was built in the early twentieth century by an eccentric Latvian immigrant named Edward Leedskalnin in memory of a lost love who jilted him at the altar. The story goes that Mr Leedskalnin, keen to prove to his old flame that he could achieve something spectacular, spent the next two or three decades building his castle, singlehandedly quarrying and sculpting 1,000,000kg of limestone coral until his magnum opus was

complete. Even his furniture was made from coral. According to legend, he only worked at night to ensure that nobody would see how he'd mastered the art of moving gigantic slabs by himself. Many of the coral stones he used were up to three times bigger than the largest stones used in the Great Pyramid of Giza, and his astonishing feat of engineering stumped even modern-day experts.

In the 1980s, it was reported in American newspapers that even the most sophisticated computer technology was unable to calculate how this 5ft man, who never weighed more than 8.5 stones, was able to carve a 9ft gate from a single slab of coral and find the exact centre of balance so it could be opened or closed with just the push of a finger.

Though Mr Leedskalnin was a private man who never revealed his secret publically, it was well known that he held many obscure theories about magnetism. In fact, several witnesses claimed to have seen the architect moving gigantic slabs of coral through the air as easily as if they were hydrogen balloons. The only clue Mr Leedskalnin offered, when asked about his methods of working, was that he used a type of mythical machine known as a 'perpetual motion holder', a contraption that most rational thinking scientists say could never exist, owing to the simple fact that it wouldn't need an external source of energy in order to function.

Whatever the secret of its construction, Coral Castle remains a popular visitor attraction to this day.

♪ Brought Home ♪

J. G.

Printed in *The Falkirk Herald and Linlithgow Journal*, 27 November 1873

I held the sea-shell to mine year,
Then gently from within did hear
Sweet murmurings, both soft and clear:
I mused most serious.
Perhaps from some far-distant sea
Comes that sweet echo o'er to me,
To thrill my soul, and ever be
A sound mysterious.

Encased within its little room,
As if imparting now my doom,
Like to a voice beyond the tomb,
It calls to me:–
As from a silent far-off shore –
The land of which we've heard of yore –
Where sound nor dip of plying oar
Ne'er greets the sea.

To that within attune thine ear,
The soul's incessant murmuring hear,
The same weird song is singing here,
As in the shell –
The music of the soul, in chime,
Uplifts the mind to thoughts sublime,
Beyond the grave and grasp of time,
And funeral knell:–

Where neither night nor day appears,
Nor weeks and months roll into years –
Where no lone one is brought in tears
To drink Death's stream.
We on this shore of time still stand,
As little marked as grains of sand
Or pebbles, strewn upon the strand,
That coldly gleam.

A Silver Fossil Shell

A miner who was employed in a silver mine in Caracoles, South America, made an intriguing discovery in about 1880. One day he dug up a large, fossilized shell that appeared to have been made out of pure silver. Astonished, he took his find straight to a jeweller, expecting to be offered a considerable sum of money. The discovery was sent away for scientific examination, but much to the disappointment of the miner it turned out to be an ordinary fossilized seashell whose calcareous surface had been replaced by a layer of silver. This was the result of natural electrotyping, which had taken place deep within the silver mine.

Stone Age Seashell Lamps

It's well known that the electric light bulb was developed by British and American scientists during the nineteenth century, replacing the oil and gas lamps of the Georgian era. Candles and simple oil lamps had been used to light the dark long before this, but exactly how long artificial lighting had been in existence was uncertain until 1939, when a historian named F.W. Robins made an astonishing revelation. He professed that Stone Age man was the earliest known human to use artificial lamps. His research showed that in about 70,000 BC, Cornish cavemen discovered it was possible to manufacture lamps out of seashells. Their unique well-like shape made an ideal reservoir for animal fat, into which a vegetable fibre wick was placed. The best type of shells for this purpose were pectin, oyster, scallop, mussel and whelk; and as humans had been proficient in making fire since at least 125,000 BC, the wicks were easy to ignite, affording a source of artificial light that lasted long into the night.

♪ Night-Songs of the Sea ♪

Printed in *The Blackburn Standard and Weekly Express*, 24 November 1888

I

A rolling, restless, moaning sea –
A flush of sundown overhead,
And waves that murmur bodingly,
With tinge of dying red;–
O sea, what words of mystery
Are these they voice hath said.

Hast thou a legend of the sleep
That comes to all at eventide? –
The sweet reposing, calm and deep,
That cannot long abide?
Or of the secret thou dost keep
In caverns undescried?

II

In midnight calm the waters lie,
With heavy, long and slumberous sound!
The steeping coast and starless sky
Are shadow-bound –

Save where with intermittent ray
The lighthouse flashes from the shore,
And crying sea-gulls through the grey
Wheel o'er and o'er.

It sends its message from the coast,
A steadfast angel of the dark,
While passes like a fleeting ghost
The fisher's bark.

III

How like a guilty self-reproachful soul
The water foams and breaks,
Whilst far beyond its everlasting roll
The glimpse of morning wakes.

Dash o'er the lighthouse, madly vexèd sea!
O gulls, awake and wail!
Yon shattered mast that quivers drearily
Proclaims a dismal tale.

And yet afar there lies another Life,
Where seas nor tempests are;
Beyond the trouble of this weary strife,
Beyond the morning star.

Poor breaking hearts, ye know not what is best,
Whose eyes are blind with tears;
How can ye see the Paradise of rest
Which lies beyond the years?

Seaweed Paper

A new process for making writing paper out of seaweed was discovered in Japan and introduced to Britain in 1887. An abundance of this aquatic weed washed up on Britain's shores every day, so it was considered a cheap and environmentally friendly material for this purpose.

The weed was boiled with carbonate of soda, and the filtered solution was treated with sulphuric acid. This yielded a viscous paste. Once this was removed, the remaining fibrous matter was turned into paper. It was claimed that this material was strong – almost untearable, in fact – and it was transparent enough for it to be used as window glass.

Seaweed paper was found to be especially good at protecting and preserving certain items of food, particularly fruit, during transit, so by 1913, food merchants were using it to wrap up their perishable goods.

The Correct Times to Eat Fish

The Victorians believed that there were some simple rules to observe before eating fish. Firstly, providing a light supper had been eaten the night before, and a good night's sleep had been experienced, a breakfast of dried or broiled fish could be enjoyed without the risk of indigestion. Kippered herrings, Finnan haddock or a salmon steak, with boiled eggs to follow, were favoured in many households, for they were tasty, wholesome and filling dishes to start the day with.

Mussels or cockles made a nice mid-morning snack; and it was considered sensible to eat a small portion of shrimps and prawns a quarter of an hour before main meals, for these were believed to aid digestion.

If meat was on the menu during the evening, nutritionists advised cooks and housewives to serve a fish starter before the main course; but it was healthier still to forget the meat and prepare a main fish course instead. For supper, boiled or fried fish was frowned upon, but a light dish of oysters, lobster or crab was a satisfying and healthy snack before bed.

♪ Day-Break ♪

J.T. Burton Wollaston
Printed in *Family Magazine*, 1880

A boat sailed out on the ebbing tide,
To toil all night for fish in the sea;
The sails were set as she floated free,
And tossed the foaming waves aside;
And the fisherman said, as he sailed away,
'I come not back till the break of day.'

The wind arose, and the sea was wild,
And the angry waves obeyed the gale;
The fisherman thought, as he furled the sail,
Of a cottage home, of wife and child;
And he said, as he toiled, 'O God, I pray
Thou wilt keep me safe till the break of day.'

The morning sun broke over the sea,
But never a boat on its bosom lay,
And all but one were in the bay;
Oh! where could the boat and the fisher be?
The fisherman's soul had sailed away
As the dawn was breaking of Endless Day.

Fish Pudding

The Victorians used to favour fish pudding, as it was a nice way to use up the leftovers of any kind of cooked fish. However, salmon, eels, mackerel, herrings and other types of oily fish were thought to be unsuitable for delicate individuals, so white, flaky fish was preferred for this recipe.

For every two tablespoonfuls of fish, one tablespoonful of breadcrumbs was added. The breadcrumbs were first soaked in a little warm milk, then strained and beaten. Next, a beaten egg and a little seasoning were stirred into the fish and breadcrumbs, and the mixture was poured into a buttered container. This was covered with a piece of greaseproof paper and steamed gently for half an hour. The pudding was accompanied by a suitable sauce, such as parsley, depending on the type of fish that was used.

Conger Eel Soup

A tasty and nutritious recipe for conger eel soup was published in *The Inverness Courier* on 13 January 1847. It instructed cooks to soak 3lb of skinned and washed conger eel in milk and water overnight. The next day the fish was put into a pan with a tablespoonful of water and heated gently over a low fire for three hours. The bones were then picked out, and a selection of herbs was added along with finely chopped vegetables: one carrot, two turnips, two onions, a stick of celery and a sprinkling of thyme were considered best. Three pints of milk were poured over the mixture, and the whole was boiled for an hour. The soup was skimmed carefully before serving.

♪ The Fisher's Return ♪

Edward Oxenford
Printed in *Family Magazine*, 1880

The white waves roar towards the shore,
And break in snow-clouds on the strand;
The wind sings loud, as though 'twere proud
To show the strength at its command.
Yet yester e'en the moon's soft sheen
Shone o'er the waters' silent breast,
And wrapt in sleep, the azure deep
Breathed but the sense of calm and rest.

But, oh, the waves are raging!
Dread war the winds are waging!
A white mist clouds the ocean,
A white mist clouds the ocean,
And my darling, and my darling, and my darling is at sea,
And my darling, and my darling, and my darling is at sea.

The night is black, the drifting rack
Flies swiftly o'er the restless sea,
But midst a lull, in splendour full,
The moon has shown a bark to me!
One moment seen beneath the sheen
Surfaced with joy my heart to fill:
I feared my Jack would ne'er come back,
But now, oh, now I know he will!

Yes, tho' the waves are raging!
And war the winds are waging!
Tho' white mist clouds the ocean,
Tho' white mist clouds the ocean,
Yet my darling, my darling, my darling comes to me!
My darling, my darling, my darling comes to me!

Fish Custard

In 1929, a discerning cook named Mrs Ireland submitted her own prize-winning fish custard recipe to the *Dundee Evening Telegraph*, which was published on 6 February.

She directed that half a pound of filleted fish was to be cut into fine pieces and placed at the bottom of a pie dish. One beaten egg was mixed smoothly with one dessertspoonful of ordinary flour and a breakfast cupful (or about 250ml) of milk. To this was added a teaspoonful of melted butter, and salt and pepper to taste, then it was poured over the fish. The whole was baked in the oven for about half an hour, and was then ready to serve.

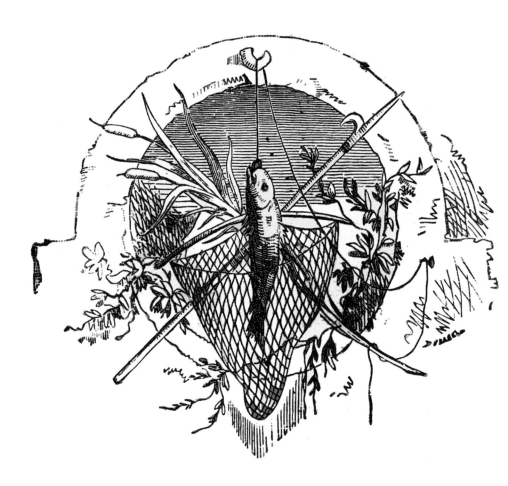

Fish Pancakes

According to a recipe in the *Portsmouth Evening News*, published on 17 June 1914, a simple and tasty dish, which could be enjoyed by all the family, was fish pancakes. To prepare a serving, two well-beaten eggs and a seasoning of salt and pepper was mixed smoothly with two dessertspoonfuls of flour and a tablespoonful of milk. Next, a teacupful of fresh, cooked fish, free from skin and bones, was stirred well into the mixture while half a tablespoonful of dripping was heating up in a pan. When hot, half of the pancake mixture was poured into the fat, and cooked until lightly browned on both sides. The pan was replenished with more dripping, in which the remainder of the pancake mixture was cooked.

♪ Sailing Home Through the Storm ♪

Charles Johns
Printed in *Family Magazine*, 1882

Homeward the fisherman steers his bark,
With shoreward bellying sail;
For the waves run high, and the night is dark,
And the fierce wind blows a gale, the fierce wind blows a gale.

No stars tonight,
No moon to light
The fisher to his home,
No! the sky is black,
As the tossing smack
Speeds swiftly over the foam
Speeds swiftly over the foam.

But little cares he for the rising sea
And little he heeds the blast;
No! he thinks of his wife and children three,
While he holds the tiller fast, he holds the tiller fast.

No storm could make
His stout heart quake,
No danger make him quail;
But well he knows
The fears of those
At home when storms prevail,
At home when storms prevail.

Louder and stronger blows the wind,
And higher runs the sea;
But he heeds not the waves that seethe behind
Or that keep him company, that keep him company.

The shore in sight!
A light! a light!
An open cottage door!
'Is that you, dear?'
'Yes, lass, I'm here!
Thank God! Thank God, once more!
Thank God! I'm here once more!'

Milk-Stewed Mackerel

The perfect way to cook mackerel, according to the Victorians, was to stew it in milk. One recipe, which appeared in *Lloyd's Weekly Newspaper* on 1 May 1898, advised placing well-cleaned mackerel into the bottom of a frying pan, which had first been rubbed with butter, and then covering it with milk. Two sliced onions, a sprig of parsley and lemon thyme, and a sprinkling of salt and pepper were added before the pan was covered with a lid and left to simmer over a low-medium heat for about twenty minutes.

When cooked, the mackerel was removed from the pan, placed on a warm dish and kept hot while a dessertspoonful of flour was stirred into the milk. A little more milk was added, if required, and this was brought to the boil for a couple of minutes before being poured over the fish. A sprinkling of fresh, finely chopped parsley completed the dish.

Fish and Egg Pasty

A popular seafood dish in the 1890s was fish and egg pasty. To make this, an oven-proof dish was covered thinly with pastry, and this was topped with small, cooked fillets of plaice or sole, the bones having been removed. They were seasoned to taste, and brushed with enough white sauce or cream to moisten them. Alternatively, a morsel of curry paste was mixed with gravy or stock until a thinnish sauce was created; this was especially favoured if the fillets had been fried or baked.

A number of boiled eggs, enough to cover the fish, were sliced and layered over the top, and another coating of sauce or cream was added. A sprinkling of herbs made a nice addition. The dish was covered with another layer of pastry and brushed with a little milk or a beaten egg before being baked in the oven until done.

♪ Fisherman's Song ♪

Printed in *The Dundee Evening Telegraph*, 6 April 1881

Oh, the fisherman's life is a dangerous life,
As he rides o'er the wave's high crest,
From the sunrise flush to the midnight hush
On the ocean's unquiet breast!
And brave and undaunted
His heart should be
Who daily dares death
On the treacherous sea.

And the fisherman's life is a lonely life;
Full slowly the hours pass by;
No whisper, no sound breaks the silence around;
No trusty companion is nigh.
Oh, loving and tender
His bride should be
Who dares for her sake
The restless sea!

Yet the fisherman's life is a noble life,
For he calls no man his lord;
And little he recks on his foam-swept decks
Of the gold that the landsmen hoard.
For fearless and brave,
Untrammelled and free,
Is the life that is passed
On the bounding sea.

Economical Shellfish Pie

Economical shellfish pie, popular in France in the 1890s, was so named because it could be varied to a great extent. Fresh crab or lobster was often chosen, and shrimps or prawns also worked well.

The selected shellfish was cooked, cut up and moistened with butter, milk, cream, fish sauce, or fish stock, or any two of these combined. About the same bulk of breadcrumbs as fish was then mixed thoroughly with the fish, along with any kind of seasoning. Salt and pepper, lemon juice or vinegar with chopped parsley or shredded anchovy, or cayenne with a hint of onion, were favoured. Some cooks liked to mix in a handful of cooked white fish with the shellfish; and a sprinkling of cheese enhanced the flavour. Once everything had been mixed together to form a sort of moist forcemeat, it was piled into a pastry-lined pie dish. This was covered with more pastry, baked in the oven and served hot.

Fish Salad a la Creole

This healthy dish was a family favourite during the 1890s, particularly in fishing villages, as it helped to liven up otherwise ordinary salads.

Any type of fish could be used, though white and flaky was preferable. First, the fish was boiled, and after it had been left to cool the bones were removed and the flesh was broken up into small pieces, enough to fill two cups. This was then mixed with one cupful of finely chopped celery; half a teaspoon of salt; a quarter teaspoon of pepper; a tablespoon of vinegar; half a tablespoon of lemon juice; and half a tablespoon of olive oil.

Then, one quart (the equivalent of two pints) of peeled and sliced tomatoes were placed in a saucepan along with ten drops of onion juice; a level teaspoon of salt; a blade of mace; four cloves; and half a teaspoon of paprika. This was cooked over a medium heat until the tomatoes were soft enough to be pressed through a sieve. A third of a cup of diluted gelatine was added to the sieved tomatoes along with one and a half tablespoons of vinegar, and the whole was stirred thoroughly.

To serve, the fish salad was heaped on to a platter and the tomato sauce was poured around it. A garnish of mayonnaise and lettuce completed the dish.

♪ Coming Home ♪

Theo Gift
Printed in *Family Magazine*, 1875

Across the turf, across the surf, across the flying foam,
Across the ice-bound Kentish hills,
The naked trees and frozen rills,
From foreign shores and foreign ills
I gaily journeyed home.

I knew the Hall was lighted all with Yule logs heaped on high;
That berries, waxen white and red,
Hung kiss-provoking overhead;
And madcap maids, none loth to wed,
Tripped lightly, sprightly by.

The stars were out, and all about the frost-flakes filled the air –
A light was in the church tower nigh,
Whence bells would ring out by-and-by.
The faces of the family
Seemed painted everywhere.

I enter in – a welcome din uprises all around;
The girls quick clustering round to greet,
And kiss me in confusion sweet –
Save May, who in the window-seat
Is lost to every sound.

For cousin Fred, with down-bent head, is whisp'ring soft and low,
While rose-red blushes swiftly chase
The white rose shadows from her face,
Like sunset in a silent place
Where lithe white lilies blow.

Well, sisters will be fickle still; and lovers have their day.
My mother's face of startled joy,
My father's welcome to his boy,
Will wake them from their sweet employ
The *bells*! 'Tis New Year's Day!

238

Glossary

AGINCOURT (the Battle of): On 25 October 1415, during the Hundred Years' War, a major battle was fought in northern France between the English and the French, who were at war over land. The French were defeated, and the Battle of Agincourt was commemorated in William Shakespeare's *Henry V*.

AJAX: In Ancient Greek mythology, Ajax was a heroic warrior who fought during the Trojan War. He is immortalized in Homer's *Iliad*.

ARDENT: HMS *Ardent* was a sixty-four-gun warship used by the Royal Navy during the Battle of Camperdown in 1797.

ARES: The god of war in Ancient Greek mythology.

ASSAYE (the Battle of): On 23 September 1803, the British East India Company defeated the much stronger Maratha Empire in the Indian village of Assaye during the Second Anglo-Maratha War. This was the first significant military victory for the Duke of Wellington, Arthur Wellesley.

B

BACON, Francis (Sir): Born in 1561, Sir Francis Bacon was an English philosopher, writer, scientist and statesman, whose scientific theories went on to revolutionize mankind's understanding of science.

BENBOW, John: John Benbow was an illustrious English officer in the Royal Navy during the seventeenth century. He helped to lead his country to glory during some of the era's most notable battles against France, including the Battle of Beachy Head in 1690, and the Battles of Barfleur and La Hogue two years later. He was also involved in the Action of August on 24 August 1702, a great sea battle that took place between the English and the French fleets off the coast of South America. Vice Admiral Benbow lost a leg during the conflict and died just over two months later.

BLACK JOKE: The *Black Joke* was an armed cutter – a small, fast vessel with a sail – that was in the service of the Royal Navy between 1795 and 1801. She was believed to have been the ship that alerted the rest of the fleet to the position of the Dutch navy prior to the Battle of Camperdown on 11 October 1797.

BLAKE, Robert: Robert Blake was an illustrious English admiral during the seventeenth century. His legendary victories at sea helped to secure England's naval supremacy, and he was dubbed the father of the Royal Navy.

BLENHEIM (the Battle of): The Battle of Blenheim, which took place in Bavaria on 13 August 1704, was fought between the English and French. Forming a major part of the War of the Spanish Succession, which lasted from 1701 to 1714, the battle ended in a victory for England and her allies.

BOHEMIA'S PLUME: According to a now discredited legend, Edward, the Black Prince, took a heraldic badge from his defeated opponent, John of Bohemia, after the Battle of Crécy in 1346. The badge depicts three white ostrich feathers; and however it came to have been adopted by the British Royal Family, it remains the heraldic symbol of the Prince of Wales to this day.

BRUTUS: *Brutus* was a seventy-four-gun warship used by the Dutch navy during the Battle of Camperdown in 1797.

BUCENTAURE: The *Bucentaure* was a French eighty-gun warship that participated in the Battle of Trafalgar on 21 October 1805. The British captured her following France's defeat, and though her crew later reclaimed her, she was wrecked in a storm two days after the battle.

C

CAESAR'S EAGLE SHIELD: In the days of the Roman Empire, the eagle was an important symbol that was often depicted on the standards of legions as well as coats of arms. Each legion had its own eagle, and the legionaries were required to guard their standard fiercely.

CAMPERDOWN (the Battle of): The Battle of Camperdown, one of England's greatest triumphs in naval history, was fought in the North Sea off the coast of Holland on 11 October 1797. The British commander, Admiral Adam Duncan, successfully captured eleven enemy ships belonging to the Dutch navy without losing any of his own.

CARTHAGE: The Tunisian city of Carthage was once the hub of an ancient civilization. It is now a World Heritage Site, attracting thousands of tourists each year.

CASTILE: The Kingdom of Castile, in modern-day Spain, was a prosperous and powerful state during the Middle Ages. In 1588, the kingdom mustered a fleet of sixteen galleons that were used to furnish the Spanish Armada.

COLLINGWOOD, Cuthbert (Lord): Lord Collingwood was a vice admiral of the Royal Navy during the seventeenth and eighteenth centuries. He is particularly remembered for his naval prowess during the Napoleonic Wars, and for fighting alongside Lord Nelson during the Battle of Trafalgar in 1805.

COLUMBUS, Christopher: Born in about 1450, Christopher Columbus was an Italian explorer and navigator, most famous for reaching the New World in 1492.

COOK, James: Captain James Cook, of the Royal Navy, was an English explorer and cartographer, famed for his many eighteenth-century expeditions around uncharted parts of the world, including Newfoundland and New Zealand.

CORUNNA (the Battle of): The Battle of Corunna was fought on 16 January 1809 between Britain and France during the Napoleonic Wars. Though there were hundreds of casualties, the British were able to rebuff the attacking French armies.

COUNT ARNALDOS: *Count Arnaldos* was the name of a sixteenth-century ballad about a magnificent Spanish galley manned by a mysterious helmsman.

CRÉCY (the Battle of): The Battle of Crécy was fought on 26 August 1346, during the Hundred Years' War. It took place on French soil between England and her allies, and a much larger force comprising French, Genoese and Majorcan troops. The English king, Edward III, emerged victorious.

CRIMP: An undesirable person who was engaged in the shanghaiing business, forcing, tricking or bribing young, eligible men to serve at sea on board merchant ships.

D

DANTE ALIGHIERI: Born in Florence in about 1265, Dante became known as one of Italy's most famous poets, and having composed some of the world's greatest pieces of literature, was considered to be the founder of the country's modern language.

DE RUYTER, Michiel: Michiel de Ruyter was an accomplished and celebrated Dutch admiral during the seventeenth century. An adversary of England's Robert Blake, de Ruyter secured numerous victories against the English and the French during the Anglo-Dutch Wars, though the first war ended in a victory for England in 1654.

DE WINTER, Jan Willem: Born in 1761, Jan Willem de Winter became a notable admiral in the Dutch navy, and was an important figure in the Napoleonic Wars. On 11 October 1797, having been appointed commander-in-chief of his fleet, he valiantly led his men into battle against the English off the Dutch coast of Camperdown (or Camperduin). Though de Winter was defeated and taken captive by the English, he earned praise and respect for upholding the honour of the Dutch flag.

DON: An honorific Spanish title, roughly translated as 'lord'. It was sometimes used as a generic term for a Spaniard.

DOUGLAS, James (Earl): Born in Scotland in about 1358, the 2nd Earl of Douglas was a powerful nobleman who led the Scots into battle against the English at the border village of Otterburn. The battle, which occurred in August 1388, resulted in victory for the Scottish raiders, but the earl was mortally wounded.

DRAKE, Francis (Sir): Sir Francis Drake was one of the most famous sea captains of the Elizabethan era. Born in England in about 1540, he rose to prominence in the late 1500s when he successfully circumnavigated the globe, and gained further recognition in 1588 when he and the Lord High Admiral, Charles Howard, secured an English victory against the Spanish Armada.

DUNCAN, Adam (Viscount): The 1st Viscount Duncan was an eighteenth-century admiral in the Royal Navy. He rose to glory in 1797 when he defeated the Dutch at the Battle of Camperdown, one of England's greatest triumphs in naval history.

E

EDGECOMBE: See Mount Edgcumbe House.

EDGEHILL (the Battle of): The Battle of Edgehill happened on 23 October 1642, during the English Civil War. The fight, between the Royalists and the Parliamentarians, was an unplanned skirmish that occurred when the two armies unexpectedly met each other in Warwickshire, resulting in a draw.

F

FAGGOT: The name of a bundle of sticks and twigs bound together to burn as fuel on an open fire.

FEROZESHAH (the Battle of): The Battle of Ferozeshah began on 21 December 1845 and ended the following day, with a clear victory for the British forces. The routed Sikh Empire was defeated in the Punjabi village of Ferozeshah, during the First Anglo–Sikh War, which lasted from 1845 until 1846.

G

GENOA'S BOW: During the Middle Ages, crossbowmen of the Genoese forces rose to prominence following their participation in the First and Third Crusades. So adept were these archers that leaders of opposing armies instructed their men to capture as many bowmen as possible and cut off their fingers. Genoese crossbowmen fought with the French army during the Battle of Crécy in 1346, but they proved no match for the English archers, who'd developed a method for keeping their longbows dry – and therefore fully operational – during wet weather.

GOLIATH: HMS *Goliath* was a seventy-four-gun warship of the Royal Navy, which was in service from 1781 to 1815, during the French Revolutionary Wars and the Napoleonic Wars. She was employed in several naval battles, including the Battle of the Nile, 1798.

GRAMPUS: The historical name for the orca, or killer whale.

HALBERDIER: The name for a soldier who carried a halberd, a large fifteenth-century axe-like weapon with a long shaft.

HARDY, Thomas (Sir): Born in 1769, Sir Thomas Hardy was a renowned officer in the Royal Navy. He played a key role during the Battle of Cape St Vincent in 1797; the Battle of the Nile the following year; the Battle of Copenhagen in 1801; and is perhaps most famously remembered for commanding HMS *Victory* during the Battle of Trafalgar in 1805. Admiral Lord Nelson was shot during the campaign and was allegedly comforted by Hardy as he lay dying on deck. Nelson's famous last words, 'Kiss me, Hardy,' have been greatly contested over the years, and never sufficiently substantiated.

HAVELOCK, Henry (Sir): Sir Henry Havelock was a celebrated major general in the British Army. He was responsible for the recapture of Cawnpore, a city in the British Raj, in 1857, when parts of India fell into the hands of insurgents.

HAWKE, Edward (Lord): The Right Honourable Lord Hawke was an eighteenth-century admiral in the Royal Navy. He served as First Lord of the Admiralty from 1766 to 1771, and prevented France from invading England in 1759 when he led his fleet to victory during the Battle of Quiberon Bay.

HAWKINS, John (Sir): Sir John Hawkins was an English naval commander and navigator during the sixteenth century. Using his skills as a shipbuilder, Hawkins helped to design the state-of-the-art ships that resisted the Spanish Armada in 1588.

HECATE: In Greek mythology, the goddess Hecate was associated with sorcery and magic. She also had a certain degree of dominion over the earth, sea and sky, and had the power to bestow blessings on families.

HELLAS: An archaic name for Greece.

HOBSON'S BAY: Hobson's Bay is the northernmost point of Port Phillip, near Melbourne, in the Australian state of Victoria.

HOMER: Homer was a celebrated author of the ancient world. His most famous works are the *Iliad* and the *Odyssey*.

HOWE, George (Viscount): Born in about 1725, the 3rd Viscount Howe was a successful brigadier general in the British Army. He commanded troops in the Seven Years' War, when Britain and her allies were at war with France, Russia and other adversaries. The war ended in 1764; the British coalition were the victors.

HOWE, William (Viscount): Born in 1729, the 5th Viscount Howe became a distinguished officer in the British Army who led the British forces during the American War of Independence, which raged from 1775 to 1783. One of his most notable victories was at the Battle of Bunker Hill during the Siege of Boston in 1775.

L

LA HOGUE (the Battle of): Following the Battle of Barfleur on 19 May 1692, the English victors pursued the defeated French fleet across the sea to Saint-Vaast-la-Hougue in the north of France. From 21 to 24 May, the two forces clashed, and the English fleet, under the command of Edward Russell, declared victory.

LAND SHARK: Also known as a 'land pirate', a land shark was a criminal who made their money by robbing sailors, or cheating them out of their valuables, while on land.

LARBOARD: A derivative of the old English word 'ladebord', meaning the side of a ship into which cargo was loaded, 'larboard' was the naval word for the left-hand side of a vessel. It was replaced by 'port' in 1844 to avoid confusion with 'starboard', the right-hand side of a ship.

LAWRENCE, Henry Montgomery (Sir): Sir Henry Montgomery Lawrence was an English brigadier general. He died defending the British Raj during the Indian Rebellion of 1857.

LEEWARD: The side (of a ship, person or building, for instance) that's sheltered from the wind. The leeward side of a ship is known as the lee side.

LEYDEN: *Leyden*, also spelt *Leijden*, was one of the warships used by the Dutch navy during the Battle of Camperdown in 1797.

MAMMON: A Biblical term denoting mankind's lust for wealth and material gain. During the Middle Ages, Mammon was often personified as a devil, using his demonic influence to lead weak men and women astray.

MARATHON (the Battle of): In 490 BC the Battle of Marathon occurred in Greece during the Persian Wars. The citizens of Athens defeated the attacking Persian army, who were driven out of the country for the next decade.

MARS: *Mars* was one of the warships used by the Dutch navy during the Battle of Camperdown in 1797.

MEEANEE (the Battle of): On 17 February 1843, 2,800 British soldiers were victorious in battle against 30,000 fighters of Sindh, in modern-day Pakistan.

MILTON, John: John Milton was one of England's most notable seventeenth-century poets, his most famous work being *Paradise Lost*.

MONARCH: HMS *Monarch* was a seventy-four-gun warship that was used by the Royal Navy during the Battle of Camperdown in 1797. She'd already participated in eight notable naval battles prior to this date, and after her final battle in 1801 she was retired from service, and broken up in 1813.

MONCK, George (Duke): Born in Devon in 1608, George Monck, the Duke of Albemarle, was a prominent seventeenth-century soldier, perhaps most well known for helping to restore the English monarchy following Oliver Cromwell's death in 1658.

MOUNSEER: An archaic spelling of the French *monsieur*; in other words, a Frenchman.

MOUNT EDGCUMBE HOUSE: Situated in Cornwall's Mount Edgcumbe Country Park, Mount Edgcumbe House was built by Richard, the first baron Edgcumbe, in about 1547. Overlooking the Plymouth Sound, the estate incorporates a chapel and lighthouse, as well as a nearby beacon site for the use of passing ships.

MYNHEER: A generic name for a Dutchman.

N

NASEBY (the Battle of): The Battle of Naseby, which took place in Northamptonshire on 14 June 1645, was a pivotal event of the English Civil War. King Charles I's army was defeated by the Parliamentary Army, commanded by Oliver Cromwell and Sir Thomas Fairfax.

NELSON, Horatio (Lord): Born in 1758, the 1st Viscount Nelson is remembered by history as one of Britain's greatest naval commanders. He was a vice admiral in the Royal Navy, and steered his fleets to victory in many maritime battles, particularly during the Napoleonic Wars. He famously lost an arm in battle before being blinded in one eye, and was ultimately killed in action as he led his men to glory at the Battle of Trafalgar, 1805.

NEREID: In Greek mythology, the Nereids were female sea nymphs who occasionally offered assistance to sailors in peril. According to the old legend, the Nereids helped Jason and his Argonauts during their voyage to Colchis to find and retrieve the Golden Fleece.

NILE (the Battle of the): From 1 to 3 August 1798, a British fleet under the command of Horatio Nelson defeated a fleet of French warships in Egypt. During the months leading up to the battle, a naval campaign between the two archenemies, Nelson and Napoléon Bonaparte, had been raging across the Mediterranean, as the French sought to invade Egypt and destabilize Britain's dominion. It culminated in this ferocious battle at AbÐ QÐr Bay.

NORE: The place where the river Thames meets the North Sea.

O

OTTERBOURNE (the Battle of): The Battle of Otterbourne, also spelt Otterburn, was a bloody skirmish that occurred between English and Scottish forces on the Scottish border. The English, led by Sir Henry 'Hotspur' Percy, were defeated by the Earl of Douglas, commander of the Scottish invaders.

P

PALOS: A town in southern Spain, and the place from where Christopher Columbus set sail in 1492, on his way to the New World.

PARK, Mungo: Mungo Park was a British explorer who ventured into the wildest regions of unexplored Africa during the late eighteenth and early nineteenth centuries.

PARRY, William (Sir): Born in England in 1790, Sir William Parry was a rear admiral in the Royal Navy, perhaps most famous for being an Arctic explorer during the early nineteenth century. In 1827 he reached the highest latitude ever attained.

PICARD FIELD: In the sixteenth century, Picardy was an administrative region in the north of France, an area close to the site of historical battles such as Agincourt and Crécy, both of which resulted in major victories for the English.

PLASSEY (the Battle of): On 23 June 1757, the British defeated French and Bengali forces in the Bengali village of Plassey, establishing a firm foothold in the region for the British East India Company. This international trading enterprise prospered until 1858, when it was nationalized.

POITIERS (the Battle of): The Battle of Poitiers occurred in France on 19 September 1356. Forming a key event in the Hundred Years' War, the battle resulted in a resounding English victory against the French forces.

POWERFUL: HMS *Powerful* was a seventy-four-gun warship used by the Royal Navy during the Battle of Camperdown in 1797.

R

REDOUBTABLE: The *Redoubtable* was a powerful warship of the French Navy. Commanded by Captain Lucas, she participated in the Battle of Trafalgar on 21 October 1805, and famously duelled with Admiral Lord Nelson's ship, HMS *Victory*. Though the British won the battle, Nelson was killed by the *Redoubtable*'s gunfire.

RODNEY, George Brydges (Baron): Born in 1718, Lord Rodney was an admiral in the Royal Navy. He commanded his men during the American War of Independence and famously led Britain to victory in the Battle of Cape St Vincent in 1780, defeating the Spanish squadron following a ferocious moonlit mêlée.

ROOKE, George (Sir): Born in Canterbury in 1650, Sir George Rooke was an admiral in the Royal Navy who commanded his troops in several notable seventeenth-century wars and battles, including the Third Anglo-Dutch War, the Battles of Barfleur and La Hogue, and the Williamite War in Ireland.

S

SALAMIS (the Battle of): The Battle of Salamis was a naval conflict that took place in Greece in 780 BC. The opposing sides were Greece and the First Persian Empire. The Persian king, Xerxes I, launched an invasion attempt, but the battle resulted in a victory for the Grecian allies.

SEMPER EADEM: A Latin phrase meaning: 'Ever the same', adopted as a motto by Queen Elizabeth I of England.

SENDAL: A type of silk-like material used during the Middle Ages to make flags, banners, fine garments, liturgical vestments and other items of worth.

SHOVELL, Cloudesley (Sir): Sir Cloudesley Shovell was an English admiral who sailed the seas during the seventeenth and eighteenth centuries. He saw action in many notable wars and battles, including the Third Anglo-Dutch War and the War of the Spanish Succession; and he was interred at Westminster Abbey following his death in 1707.

SIDON: Once a thriving commercial centre of the ancient world, Sidon is a coastal city in present-day Lebanon. It was an important place in Biblical times, as Jesus supposedly visited.

SPANISH ARMADA: In 1588, a fleet of 130 ships sailed from Spain to England, with the intention of invading the country. As soon as the enemy ships were spotted, beacons were lit across England to warn citizens of the approaching threat. Queen Elizabeth I responded by mustering her own naval fleet, led by some of England's finest naval commanders, including Francis Drake, Lord Howard of Effingham and John Hawkins. The Spanish were ultimately defeated, partially because of the poor weather conditions off the English coast.

ST VINCENT: The Battle of Cape St Vincent took place on 14 February 1797 off the coast of Portugal. It was one of the earliest battles during the

Anglo-Spanish War, which lasted from 1796 until 1808. Horatio Nelson helped to lead the British to victory; the much larger Spanish fleet was defeated.

T

TEXEL: Texel is an island and municipality in the north of Holland, a place that bore witness to plenty of naval action during the Anglo-Dutch Wars, the Napoleonic Wars, the American Revolution and the two world wars.

TRAFALGAR (the Battle of): The Battle of Trafalgar, one of Britain's most memorial naval triumphs, occurred on 21 October 1805, during the Napoleonic Wars. The two opposing sides were Britain, under the command of Horatio Nelson and Lord Collingwood, and the combined fleets of Spain and France. The battle ended with a resounding British victory, but Admiral Lord Nelson paid with his life.

TRINIDADA: The *Trinidada*, otherwise the *Santísima Trinidad*, was a state-of-the-art and heavily armed Spanish warship that participated in the Battle of Trafalgar in 1805. Though she was much larger than Horatio Nelson's ship, HMS *Victory*, she was no match for the British fleet, and was captured on 21 October, but sank in a violent storm the following day.

TRIUMPH: HMS *Triumph* was a seventy-four-gun warship used by the Royal Navy during the Battle of Camperdown in 1797.

TROLLOPE, Henry (Sir): Sir Henry Trollope was a British officer of the Royal Navy in the eighteenth and nineteenth centuries. During the Battle of Camperdown, which took place off the coast of Holland on 11 October 1797, he commanded the seventy-four-gun sailing ship, *Russell*, and was later knighted for his bravery following the defeat of the Dutch fleet.

TYRE: An ancient coastal city in modern-day Lebanon, once part of the great Roman Empire. It was said that Jesus visited the region in Biblical times, where he healed the sick and preached to the masses.

V

VAN TROMP, Maarten (Admiral): Maarten Van Tromp, also known as Maarten Tromp, was a Dutch naval commander in the seventeenth century.

He was alleged to have attached a broom to his ship's mast to symbolize his intention of sweeping the English out of the sea. His adversary, Robert Blake, reputedly responded by attaching a whip to his ship's mast, signifying his plan to whip the Dutch fleet from the waves.

VITORIA (the Battle of): Also spelt Vittoria, the Battle of Vitoria took place on Spanish soil on 21 June 1813. The British and allied forces, led by the Duke of Wellington, defeated the French army; it was an event that led to an allied victory during the Peninsular War.

VRYHEILD: The *Vryheild* was a Dutch flagship that was involved in the Battle of Camperdown in 1797. When she surrendered to the English, a number of artefacts, including her figurehead, were taken as trophies by the victors.

W

WATERLOO (the Battle of): Arguably one of the most famous battles in English history, the Battle of Waterloo was fought in the Netherlands, now Belgium, on 18 June 1815. The Duke of Wellington led troops of the Seventh Coalition to victory against Napoléon Bonaparte's French forces.

WATT, James: James Watt was a British scientist and engineer. His pioneering inventions, notably his steam engine, were fundamental in bringing about the Industrial Revolution, which lasted from about 1760 until about 1840. The electrical watt was named after him.

WELLINGTON, the Duke of, Arthur Wellesley: The 'Iron Duke' was born in Dublin in 1769, and was one of Britain's most prominent political and military figures of the nineteenth century. As an officer in the British Army, he rose to prominence during the Napoleonic Wars, and is most remembered for his defeat of the eponymous French leader, Napoleon.

WHEATSTONE, Charles (Sir): Born in 1802, Sir Charles Wheatstone was one of Britain's most successful inventors of the Victorian era. He was also a scientist, playing a key role in the development of telegraphy and electrical engineering.